Ruth Artmonsky

DO YOU WANT IT GOOD OR DO YOU WANT IT TUESDAY?

The halcyon days of
W.S. Cowell Ltd. Printers

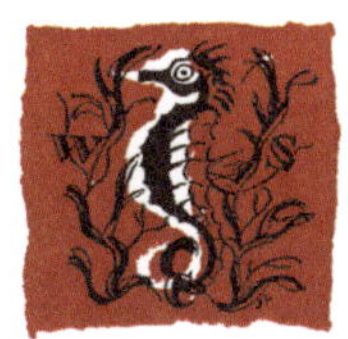

W. S. COWELL LIMITED
23 PERCY STREET
LONDON W1

Telephone
MUSEUM 9166

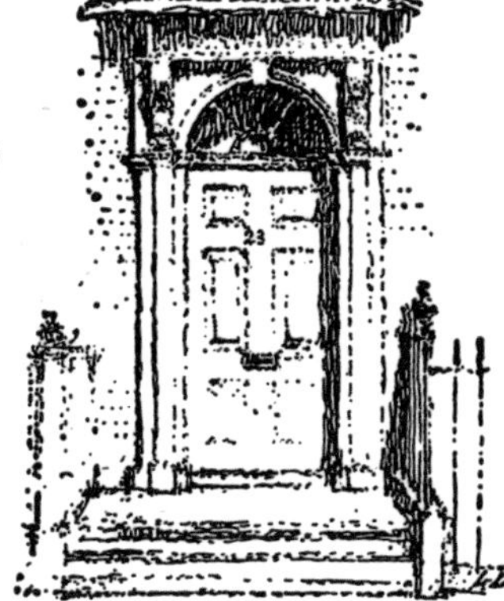

W. S. COWELL LIMITED
BUTTER MARKET
IPSWICH

Telephone
IPSWICH 2276

Published by Artmonsky Arts
Flat 1, 27 Henrietta St.
London WC2E 8NA
Telephone 020 7240 8774
Email ruthartmonsky@yahoo.co.uk

ACKNOWLEDGEMENTS
My thanks go to Suffolk Record Office, which holds the W.S. Cowell Ltd. archive; and to the many retired Cowell employees and their relations, who gave so generously of their time and loaned material.

ISBN 978-0-9551994-7-9

Designed by Webb & Webb Design Limited
Printed in England by J. W. Northend Ltd.

CONTENTS

Introduction *7*

Part One **A History** *11*

Part Two **Illustrated Book Works** *23*

Babar the Elephant *25*

Ardizzone and the Little Tim Books *29*

Kathleen Hale and Orlando, the Marmelade Cat *32*

The Puffin Picture Books *38*

Ravilious and Submarine Dream *47*

John Lewis and A Handbook of Printing Types *50*

The School Prints *57*

The Aldeburgh Festival Programme *64*

The Royal Philatelic Collection *69*

The Place of Crowning *72*

David Gentleman and the Limited Editions Club *77*

Wild Flowers of The United States *84*

Chalk Magazine *89*

Epilogue *93*

Bibliography *95*

Appendix One **Autolithographic Progress and Plastic Film by Geoffrey Smith** *96*

Appendix Two **Autolithography of Plastic Plates by Noel Carrington** *102*

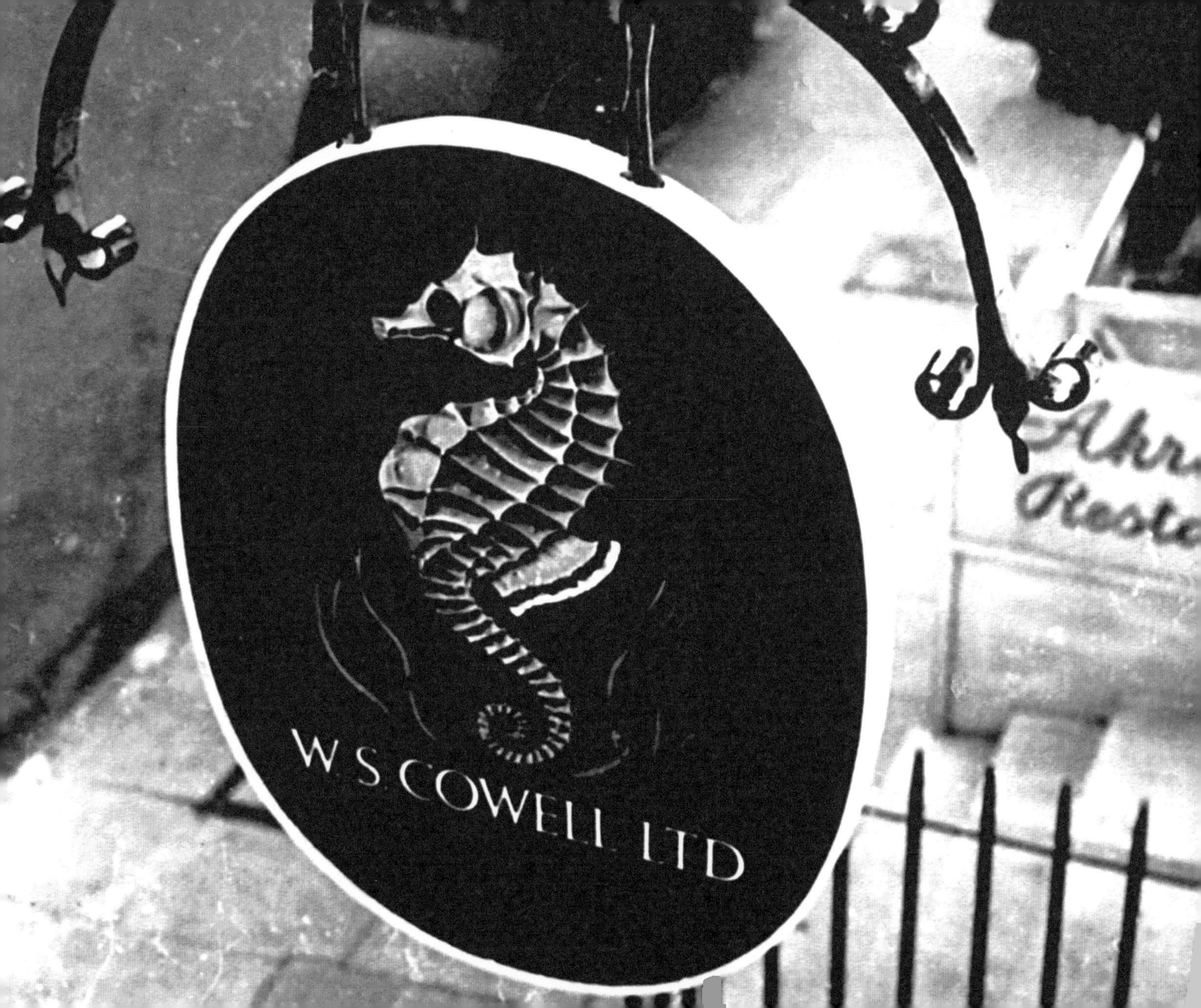
W. S. COWELL LTD

Ruth Artmonsky

INTRODUCTION

I first came across W.S. Cowell Ltd. when writing about *The School Prints,* a madcap adventure in which a young debutante hauls Geoffrey Smith, a Director of Cowells, across France, to persuade the likes of Picasso, Dufy, Leger and Matisse to produce works for British school children. I was momentarily intrigued by the thought of a provincial printer swooping across France in a small plane to meet the masters. As my focus was on the young debutante I foolishly accepted a report, without further checking, that Cowell's records had been destroyed when the firm was sold.

Imagine my surprise and delight when, some years later, I was handed a somewhat worn file containing over one hundred and thirty letters from the great and the good of the British publishing and art world, obviously collected together by Cowells, which they had received in response to their publicity for a book of types, compiled by John Lewis in 1948. The file was to be lodged in Lewis's archives in Reading University. I wrote a quick note, to be added to

Cowell sign in Percy Street - *designed by Roland Collins*

the file, explaining the circumstances of Lewis writing the book, and summarising the content of the response letters.

It only took a little more perseverance than that I had shown when writing *The School Prints* for me to discover that not only were Cowell's archives NOT destroyed, but that they were in fact well archived in the Suffolk Record Office in Ipswich. A thorough perusal of these archives crushed any London snobbery of Cowells as a provincial printer, and revealed that, for a halcyon period, from the 1930s to the 1960s, Cowells had been at the fore of their industry, particularly when it came to colour printing.

As my interests have tended to lie with the 'unacknowledged' in creative projects, (people behind events who are overshadowed by more noisy frontmen), it was inevitable that Cowells was to be the next cause to be championed. I was particularly interested in the relationships of key Cowell's personalities with their commissioning publishers, artists, designers, or madcap debutantes.

John Lewis, in a later book – *A Handbook of Type and Illustration* – hints at some of the 'human' problems in printing, additional to technical ones:

> 'It is a sad fact that if illustrations are not ruined by poor reproduction or the use of an unsuitable process, they are often spoiled by unfortunate placing on the paper, or by juxtaposition of an inappropriate typeface. In addition to this, one of the many reasons for unsuccessful graphic reproduction is that illustrators are often bemused by the beauty of their original work, and give little thought to what it may look like when it is reproduced. This attitude is not helped by the unsympathetic approach of many printers, publishers and block makers towards drawings that at first sight may appear unsuitable for reproduction.'

Geoffrey Smith, Cowell's joint managing director during its 'halcyon' days, the most amenable of characters, saw nothing but sheer delight in the possibility of working with publishers and illustrators to produce high quality illustrated books and his first experience of printing for Methuens, the first British translation of the *Babar* books, did nothing to dispel his optimism. It only encouraged him further to establish his company in this market; and, during his stewardship, Cowells was to produce, on a commercial basis, some of the best illustrated books of the period, particularly for children.

This book is meant as a general reader in illustrated book printing; but, for those more technically inclined, relevant appendices have been included. The body of the book describes some of Cowell's key book productions; a comprehensive list of all the books they printed remains to be researched.

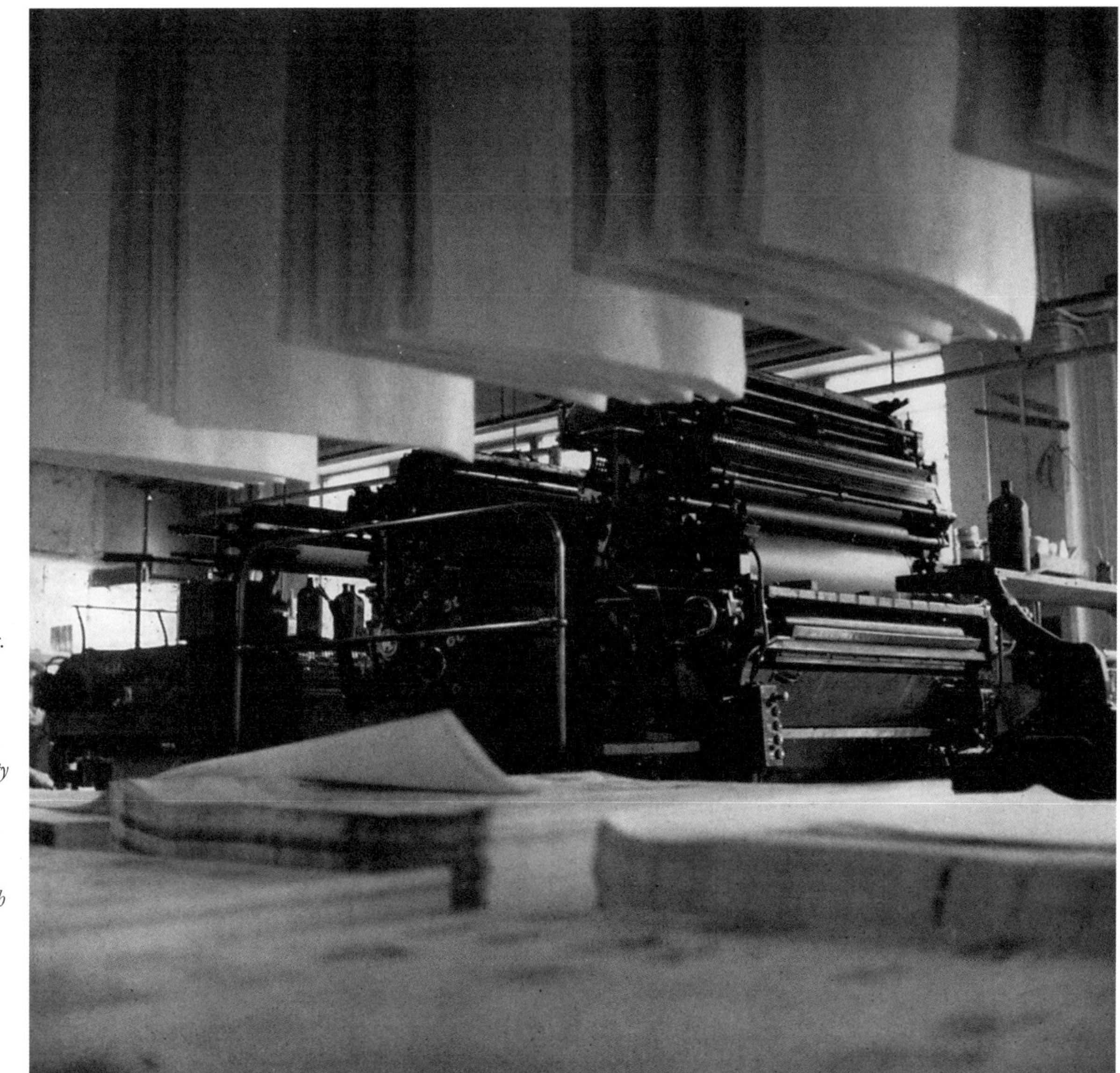

W.S. Cowell printing press. '…or paper hanging from a slowly moving overhead railway maturing, reaching the exact degree of humidity and temperature of the machine room – a necessity for exact register in offset colour printing'. Photograph by Geoffrey Ireland, 1960 from The Press in the Butter Market

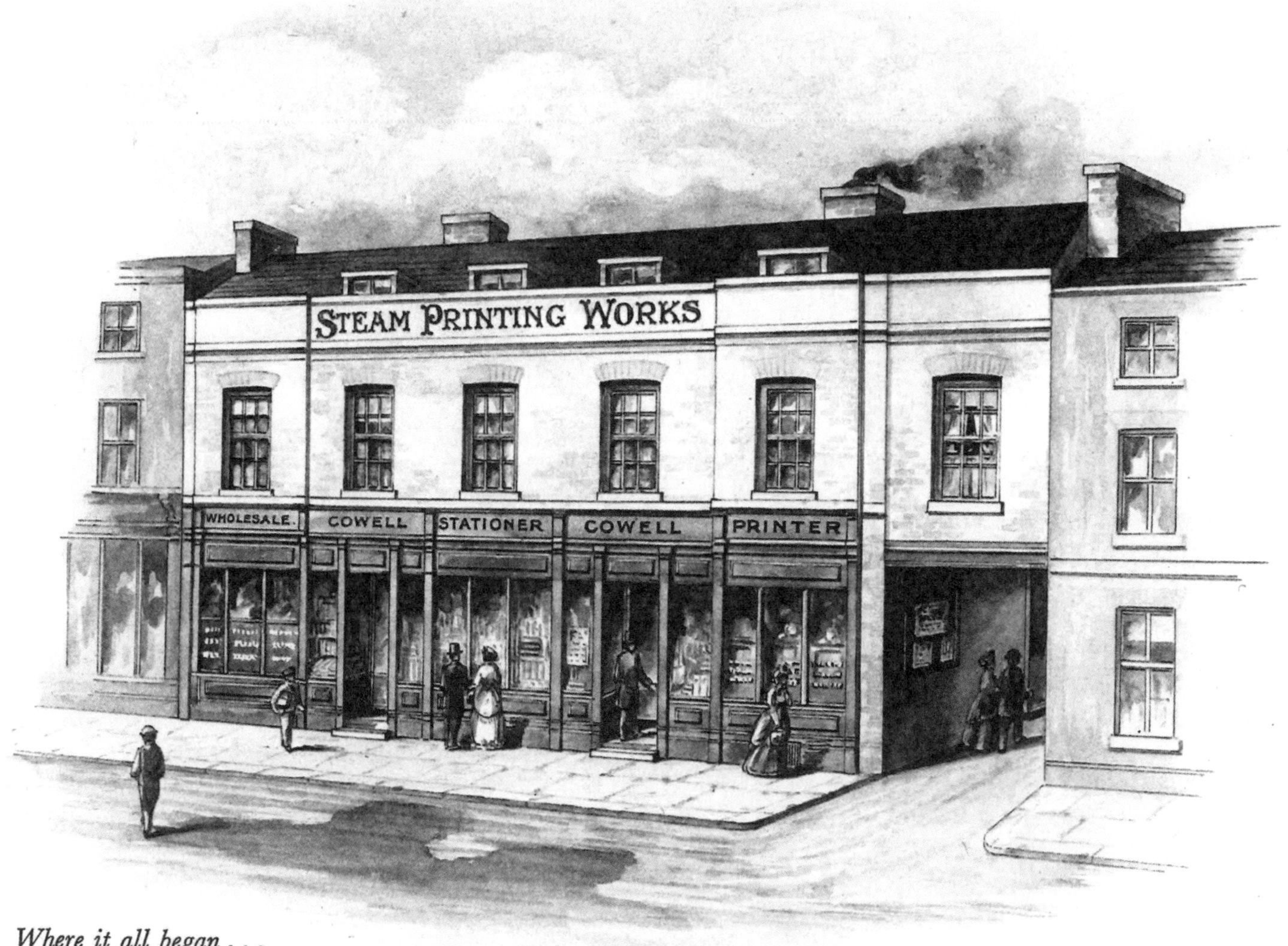

Where it all began . . .

Part One

A HISTORY

The history of W.S. Cowell Ltd. can be seen as the story of two dynasties – the Cowells, who started the firm in 1818 and had controlling shares until 1923, and the Hansons, one of whom joined the firm in 1866, and like a cuckoo in the nest, worked his way in, his family taking full control of the company by the early 1920s. The Smiths enter the picture at the turn of the century when one, R.W. Smith, married a Hanson daughter.

By 1800, the Butter Market had become one of the main commercial streets in Ipswich. In 1818, Abraham Kersey Cowell, a local corn merchant, set up his second son, S.H. Cowell, then eighteen, as a printer and stationer, at number ten. The father, an enthusiastic Baptist, had seen the potentiality of a market for religious tracts, and by 1823, his son was profitably printing hymn books. Additionally, he took over an adjoining property, starting a short-lived tea and coffee business, and an altogether more successful wine and spirits on and off-licence that survived until

1953. In time, a retail store was added, selling not only stationery, but travel goods, toys and household goods; this was eventually hived off in 1963.

Cowells, the printers, although based in Ipswich, was from the start striving to be ahead of its rivals nationally and by the mid-19th century had established a reputation for itself for printing by lithography. This had been invented in 1796 by Alois Senefelder as a cheap method of printing, using a stone or metal plate. That it was an effective means of printing artwork as well as texts was particularly attractive to Cowells.

They also became one of only four British printers licensed to use a German process – Anastatic printing which made use of transfer paper rather than stone or plate. Cowells was able to exploit the market for artists who wanted their work printed, by supplying artists with the special paper, along with litho-drawing ink and crayon. Artists returned their completed work to Cowells for transferring on to stone for impressions to be made. Soon a national Anastatic Drawing Society was founded, of which Cowells were the sponsors – a happy combination for them of 'doing good' and profiting thereby.

And Cowells were intent to stay ahead when it came to mechanisation, introducing power steam engines by the second half of the century, electricity by the 1880s, and a two-colour press machine by 1875. A Cowell's publicity booklet of the time listed their possessing Wharfedales, a two-colour Newsum, several platens, a hot rolling machine, and six flat-bed lithographic machines. A Monotype machine was installed shortly after its invention. Eric Hanson, a grandson of the first Hanson at Cowells, recorded 'there was never any holding back from the installation of the most modern machinery and equipment.' By the 1920s all the Works' machines had their own electric motors, and the Directors were travelling across Europe, and to America, continually looking for the latest developments. By the mid-20th century most processes had been mechanised, hot metal casting having given way to photo-typesetting, and the umpteen hand-worked bindery tasks being replaced by a one hundred foot German machine run by a few operators.

But the fact that Cowells built up a considerable reputation as colour printers was not merely a matter of advanced machinery and processes, but of taking on board people with energy and vision. By 1866, S.H. Cowell was sixty-six, and with civic duties (he was twice mayor of Ipswich) along with his business responsibilities, he looked for someone to act as aide. His own son, Walter Samuel, was

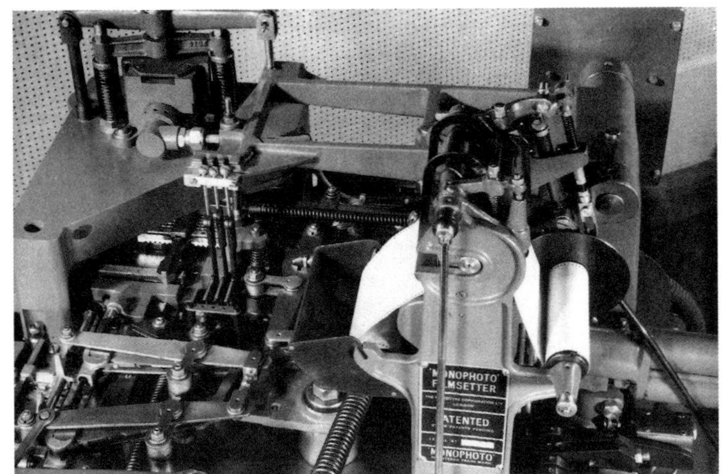

Introduction to filmsetting – a Monophoto filmsetter, 1964

seen to have rather limited business acumen, and his second son, Arthur, was mentally handicapped. An advertisement was placed for an office manager – to give orders to workmen, administer wages, supervise timekeeping, and generally make themselves useful. The annual salary offered was forty to forty-five pounds plus bed and breakfast on the company premises. William Bonser Hanson, a young man of twenty-four, from Lincolnshire, after having his religious credentials approved, joined the company, and was not long in 'making himself useful'; in fact he rapidly made himself indispensable! By 1875 he was virtually managing the operational side of the printing and stationery business. The Hanson dynasty was to thrive as that of the Cowells waned.

Towards the end of the century more properties were acquired along the Butter Market, with some rebuilding and a general rationalisation. And the ownership of the company was retitled W.S. Cowell Ltd., with the shares lying largely with W.S. Cowell but the Hansons now also having shares. W.S. Cowell was nominal head of the company, its Chairman, but W.B. Hanson was Managing Director, and his son, Harry (who had joined Cowells in 1889) was starting on the path of himself becoming Director on the death of his father in 1916. This was about the same time as R.W. Smith, Hanson's son-in-law (who had joined the firm in 1908) being made Co-Director; the cuckoos had taken over the nest.

However, it was with Smith's son Geoffrey (joined 1921) and Harry Hanson's sons Cyril (joined 1923) and Eric (joined 1934) that Cowell's 'halcyon' days began. Geoffrey, in charge of sales, and Cyril, in charge of the Works, had both been trained at the London College of Printing, and, although this was clear nepotism, both brought a new energy and professionalism to the firm. They worked in tandem

FAMILY TEA,

Coffee, and Spice Warehouse,

NEW MARKET LANE,

BUTTER MARKET, IPSWICH.

S. H. COWELL

Begs very respectfully to acquaint his Friends and the Public, he has opened a Shop, adjoining his present business, for the Sale of GENUINE TEAS, COFFEE, and SPICES. At the last Sale it is well known a great reduction took place in the price of Tea, and S. H. C. has been enabled to purchase his Entire Stock, direct from the East India Company's Warehouses, on the most advantageous terms. He pledges himself to give the full benefit of it to the consumer, who has now an opportunity of purchasing Tea, cheaper than has been offered to the public for the last 15 years. S. H. C. solicits attention to the following Prices, for Ready Money only.

	Per Pound. s.	d.		Per Pound. s.	d.
Good Bohea	3	8	Very Fine Souchong	10	0
Good Congou	5	0	Strong Caper	8	0
Fine Rough ditto	5	4	Fine Pekoe	11	0
Ditto	5	8	Fine Bloom	7	6
Ditto	6	0	Good Hyson	8	0
Good Souchong	6	8	Fine ditto	10	0
Fine ditto	7	0	Super ditto	12	0
Ditto	8	0	Strong Gunpowder	13	0
Good Plantation Coffee	2	0	Sir Hans Sloane's Chocolate	6	0
Fine Jamaica ditto	2	6	Best Plain ditto	5	0
Ditto Berbice ditto	3	0	Plain ditto	4	0
Fine Turkey ditto	3	6	White's Cocoa	3	4

Spices of every description on the most Reasonable Terms.

☞ **No Credit Given.**

Advertisement for S.H. Cowell's shop which sold tea, coffee and spices

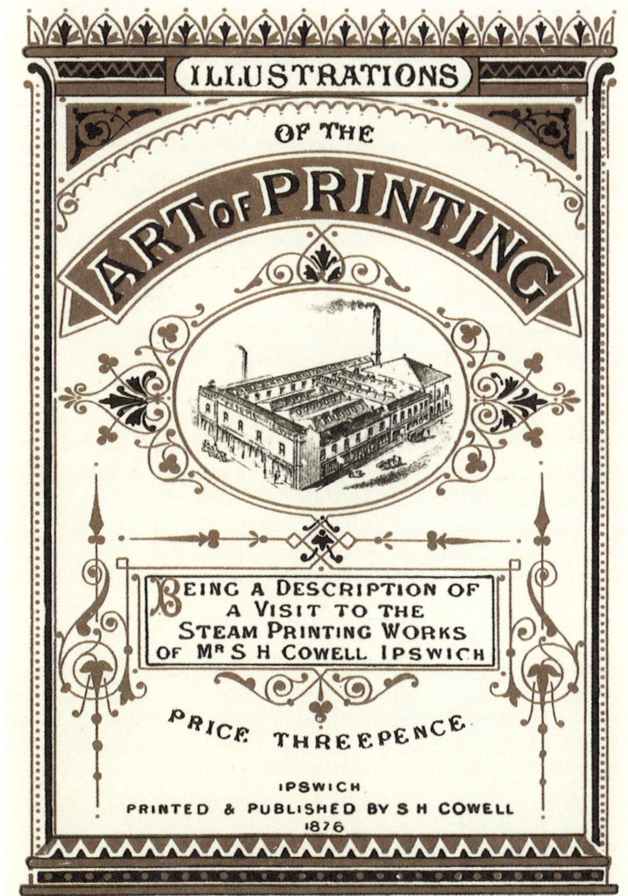

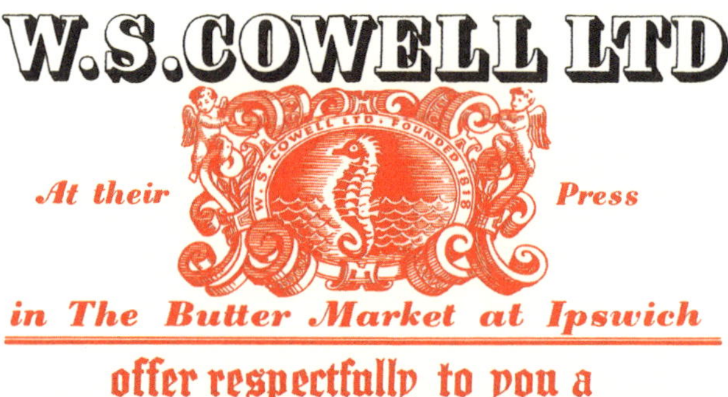

Souvenir brochure given by S.H. Cowell to visitors to his factory, 1876 (left),
W.S. Cowell Ltd. Advertising Poster, September 1947 (right)

as joint Managing Directors, and were, luckily, close friends. Unfortunately, Cyril died in a shooting accident in 1940, but Eric, who had trained as a chartered accountant, became a formidable figure, working alongside Smith in taking the company forward.

In World War Two all the younger Cowell's employees were called up into the forces; Eric was to have a key appointment with the Ministry of Supply. It was said that Geoffrey Smith was the only family member left to cope with a reduced staff, paper rationing, reduction in publishing and strict economy standards for materials being used. However, although not recorded, Eric would conscientiously keep abreast of the finances, as well as he could, at weekends and whenever his official duties allowed it.

Cowells was rapidly drawn into printing a variety of stationery for the armed forces, and booklets, in German, for the Political Intelligence Division of the Foreign Office. An archived envelope, containing examples of Cowell's war work, had written on it:

> 'Delivered to Germany by the RAF free of import licence and without customs examination at frontier.' (1943)

This refers to the fact that the little booklets were dropped by plane over Belguim and Holland, along with such Cowell printed oddities as portraits of King Leopold and Queen Wilhemina, to encourage the resistance movement.

But Cowells can be said to have survived World War Two by Bingo! They had, pre-war, done a considerable amount of publicity work for C.H. Bernard & Sons Ltd. of Harwich, who were naval outfitters to the Fleet. The Admiralty had discovered that the playing of Tombola relaxed the troops waiting in the Mediterranean.

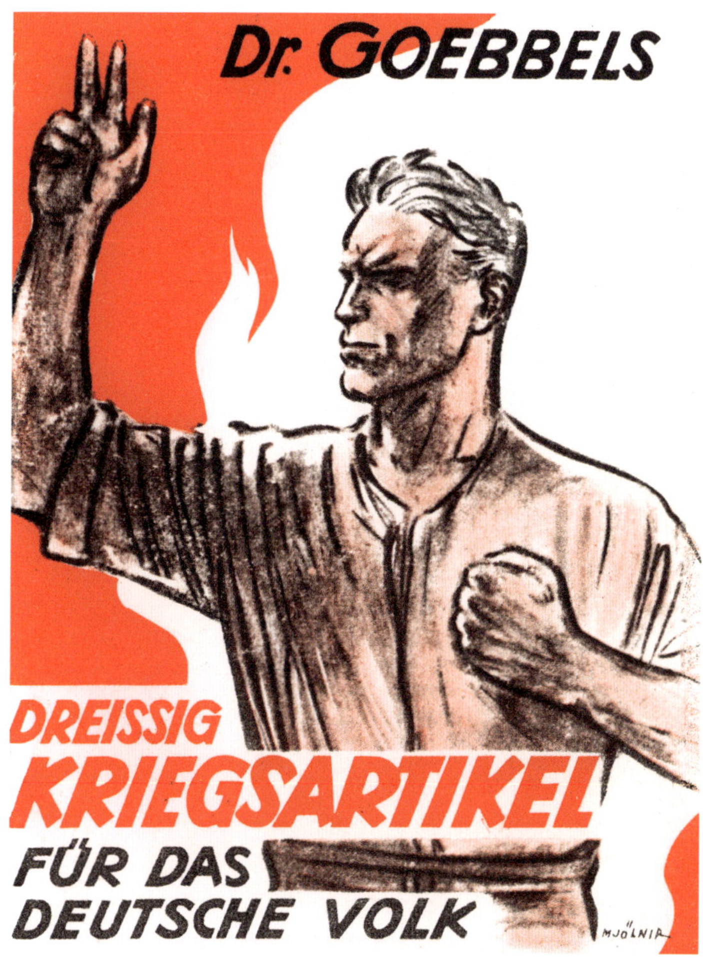

German advertising campaign, c.1943

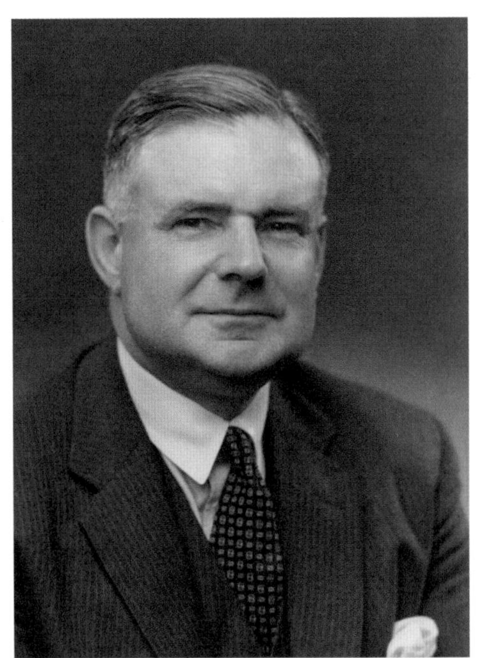

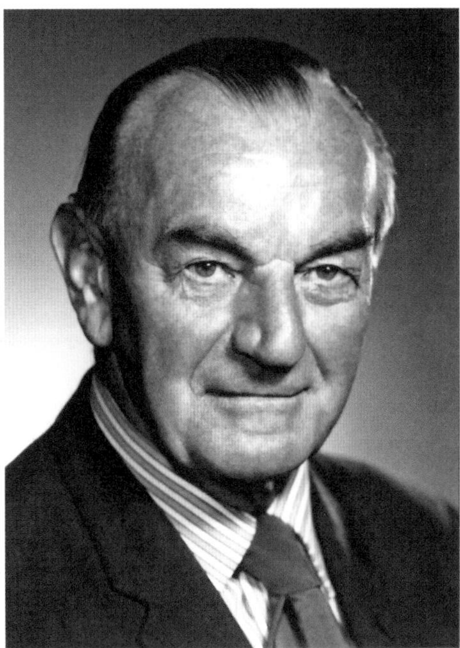

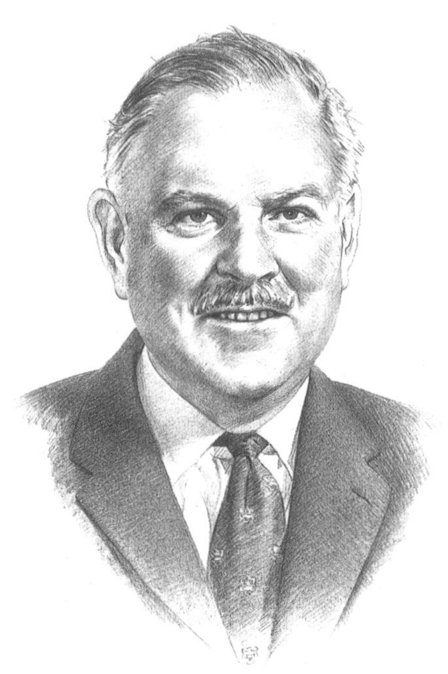

Eric Hanson, Geoffrey Smith, and Geoffrey Scott

Bernards, astutely, had acquired the copyright of the numerical combinations used in Tombola, and placed the printing of the tickets with Cowells. On the plea of 'troop welfare', and with the support of the Admiralty, Cowells was enabled to get a sufficient supply of paper for the work. Bingo, although helping out during the war, was unfortunately, as it turned out, the sole survivor when the firm's 'halcyon days' came to an end.

Eric Hanson, both charitably and modestly, wrote of Smith's sterling role during the war:

> 'Supported by S.F. Watson and W. Cooper in London, by the Associate Directors C.H. Grimmond and by Lt. Col. Horsfield, and by his keen and loyal staff, he effectively led the company through the many difficulties, so that at the end of the war it was essentially in good shape, and ready to take advantage of the opportunities which would arise after cessation of hostilities.'

But it was Hanson who had had the foresight to buy up land for possible expansion, and to buy houses to subsidise returning workers. Smith and Hanson, early in 1945, began to plan the post-war future of Cowells. They prepared a booklet – 'Your Post-War Job' – which they sent out to all their pre-war employees. The response to this ensured a sufficient workforce for carrying out their plans, which included the building of a new factory – a six-floor works opened in 1948. A new London sales office was set up at 23 Percy Street, just off Tottenham Court Road. Geoffrey King, who had worked under Geoffrey Smith as a printing representative pre-war, was appointed Sales Director. And another of Smith's protégées, George Bodley Scott (ex-Marlborough and a Lt. Colonel) was appointed Works Manager. With Eric Hanson back from the Ministry, all was in position for post-war expansion.

Smith, Hanson and Scott were very different personalities who nevertheless complemented each other so well in their skills and interests as to build a 'dream team'.

Smith was the most charming of men, good-tempered, with a vast social network. It is said he knew every employee by name, and exuded warmth around the works. The tale is told that he had a sign affixed to the back of his car which lit up to say 'thank you' when he was allowed to overtake! His success in attracting work to Cowells was by a gentlemanly diplomacy and a solid technical know-how. And his aesthetic interests, although perhaps a shade conservative, were what powered Cowells to build its reputation for illustrated bookwork.

Eric Hanson, unfairly, gets an altogether lesser press, for his reserved, rather introverted personality led him to be considered remote and aloof. Yet his concern for others was to show itself in his consideration of the workforce and in his many charitable works for Ipswich and the surrounding community, as well as his concern for his profession (he was a founder member of the Institute of Printers and was much involved in the Printing Industry Federation). He was in fact a strong, determined character, with an acute financial sense, and this made him an excellent administrator and financial controller.

Geoffrey Bodley Scott was described as having a military presence – tall, well-built and brisk in manner – and would do his daily rounds in a white coat, showing he meant business, alert to everything going on. Yet Scott, like Hanson, had his softer side for

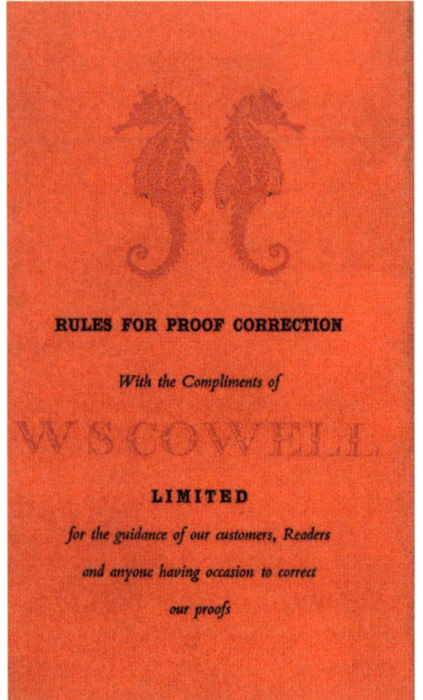

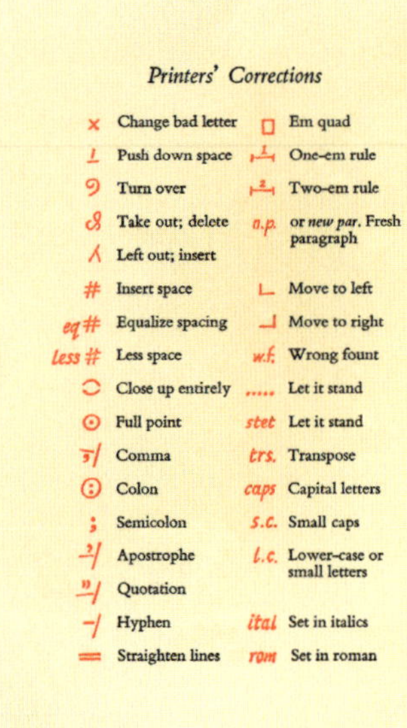

Printers' Corrections

Mark	Meaning	Mark	Meaning
×	Change bad letter	□	Em quad
⊥	Push down space	⊢1⊣	One-em rule
9	Turn over	⊢2⊣	Two-em rule
∂	Take out; delete	n.p.	or *new par.* Fresh paragraph
⋏	Left out; insert		
#	Insert space	∟	Move to left
eq #	Equalize spacing	⊣	Move to right
less #	Less space	w.f.	Wrong fount
⊂	Close up entirely	.....	Let it stand
⊙	Full point	stet	Let it stand
,/	Comma	trs.	Transpose
⦂	Colon	caps	Capital letters
;	Semicolon	s.c.	Small caps
ʼ/	Apostrophe	l.c.	Lower-case or small letters
"/	Quotation		
-/	Hyphen	ital	Set in italics
=	Straighten lines	rom	Set in roman

Proof showing correction signs

The Inland Printer prints an a musing letter from Mr T. B. Aldrich to Prof. E. S. Morse, ex-president of tqe American Academy for the Advance ment of Science. Prof. Morse it should be stated, has a handwriting quite in describable. 'My dear Morse: It was very pleasant for me to get a letter from you other the day. Perhaps I should nave found it pleasanter if I had been able to decipher it I don't think I mastered anyting beyond the date (which I knew), and the signature (which I guessed at). There's a singuliar and perpetual charm in a letter of your it never grows old; it never losesits novelty.

One can say to one's self every morning There's that letter of morse's; I haven't read it yet. I think I'll shy another take at it today and maybe I hall be able, in course of a few years, so make out what he means by those t's that look like w's, and those is that haven't any eyebrows!" Other letters are read and forgotten, but yours are kept forever—unread. One of them will last a reasonable man a lifetime Admiringly yours, T. B. Aldrich.'

initial / *caps* / s.c./⊂/ / 9/ / eq#/ / ,/ / -/ / stet/ / trs/ / h/ / eq#/ / ⊙/-/ / h/ / ×/ / ∂/ / ;/ / #/ / run on / ⊙/ʼ/ / M/ / #/ / trs/ / w.f./ / ⊂/ / ʼ/ / =/ / rom/ / ⊙/-/ / thrown away and/

Corrected Proof

THE INLAND PRINTER prints an amusing letter from Mr T. B. Aldrich to Prof. E. S. Morse, ex-president of the American Academy for the Advancement of Science. Prof. Morse, it should be stated, has a handwriting quite indescribable. 'My dear Morse: It was very pleasant for me to get a letter from you the other day. Perhaps I should have found it pleasanter if I had been able to decipher it. I don't think I mastered anything beyond the date (which I knew), and the signature (which I guessed at). There's a singular and perpetual charm in a letter of yours; it never grows old; it never loses its novelty. One can say to one's self every morning: "There's that letter of Morse's; I haven't read it yet. I think I'll take another shy at it today and maybe I shall be able, in the course of a few years, to make out what he means by those t's that look like w's, and those i's that haven't any eyebrows!" Other letters are read and thrown away and forgotten, but yours are kept forever—unread. One of them will last a reasonable man a lifetime. Admiringly yours, T. B. Aldrich.'

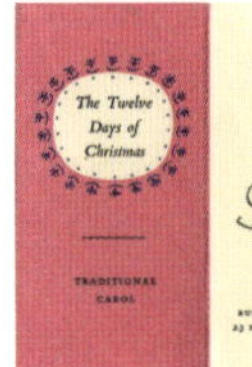

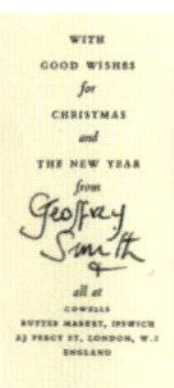

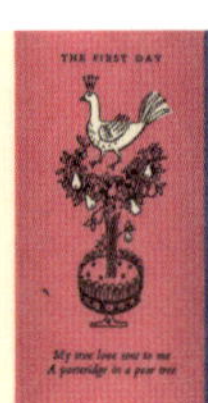

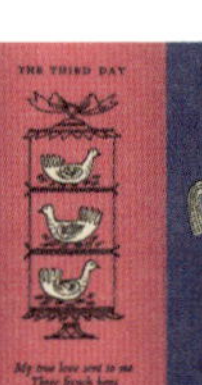

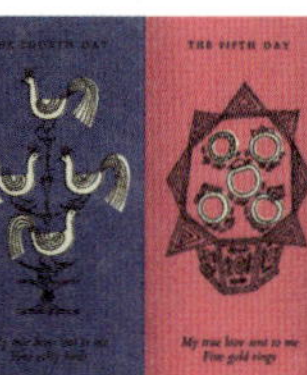

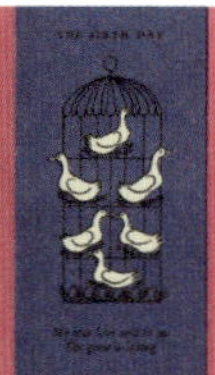

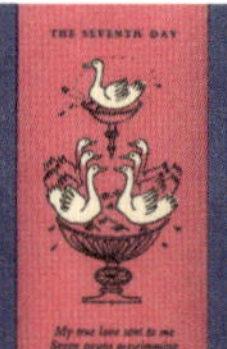

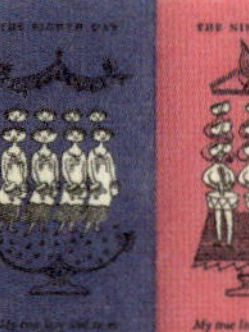

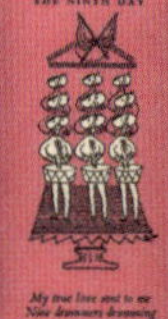

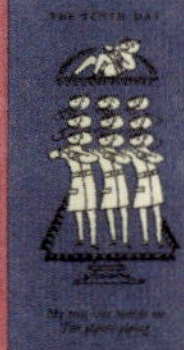

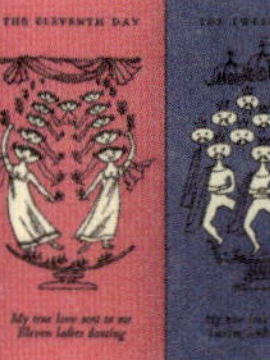

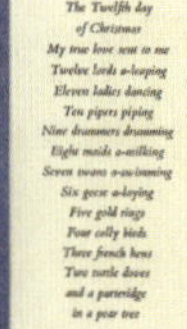

Rules for Proof Correction *by W.S. Cowell Ltd., (above), and* The Twelve Days of Christmas *Christmas card from Geoffrey Smith printed by W.S. Cowell Ltd. (below)*

he had a considerable aesthetic streak and a brilliant eye for effects. He had restored a mediaeval house, the Old Neptune, which he made available for many Cowell's social events, and is said to have hand-built panels for the local Masonic Hall.

The three managed Cowells when it was on a crest of a wave and their pride in the firm's work cascaded down to their workforce who were led to believe that Cowells was the best and that their contribution, however small, was crucial. A Cowell's staff handbook gives a flavour of the spirit the three of them conjured up:

> 'Over many years W.S. Cowell Ltd. has built up a reputation for high quality work in letterpress and offset printing and in the finishing processes. This reputation depends on the care with which each person concerned does his own particular part in producing a job.'

Cowells had, just prior to, and at the beginning of, the war, started to print some coloured children's books – the first English edition of *Babar the Elephant*, Kathleen Hale's first *Orlando, the Marmalade Cat* books, and, edited by Noel Carrington, the first Puffin Picture Books. Smith was determined, by further similar projects, to take his company into high quality book production. They were already established colour printers, and now, with the help of their invention of Plastocowell sheets, a great grandchild of Anastatic printing, they began to attract a flurry of artists and publishers to Ipswich. The halcyon days were in full flood, and *Barbar, Orlando* and the Puffins were to be followed, for some thirty years, by dozens of other colourful productions.

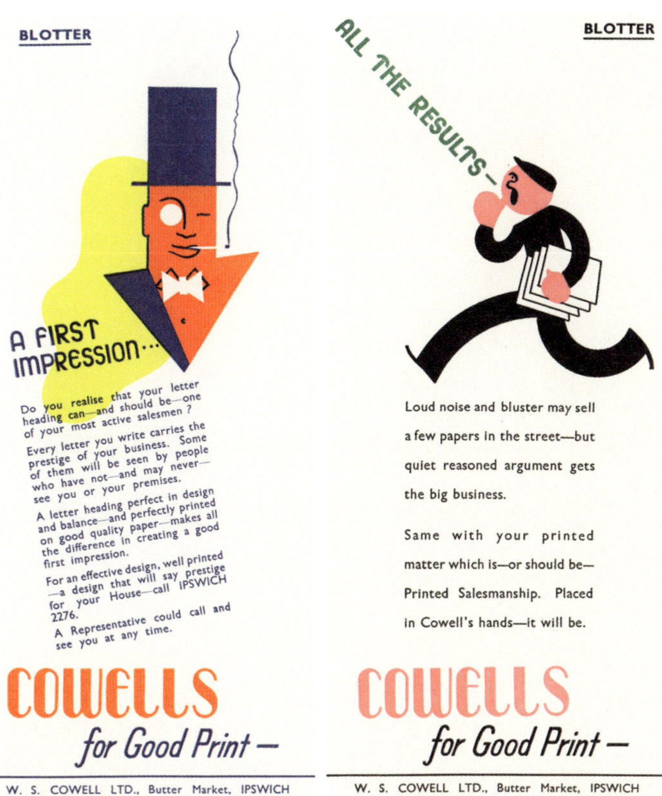

Two examples of Cowell's advertising blotters

However, by the late sixties, Smith and Hanson were running down to retirement. Two nephews were brought in, but one, Charles, decided his future lay in academia, whilst the other, David, although cutting his teeth in printing at Cowells, being trained at the London College of Printing, and learning the toughness and competitiveness necessary for print selling and for delivering to schedule, decided to make his own way, elsewhere, eventually running his own printing business.

In 1964, the whole equity of the company was bought by Grampian Holdings Ltd. on condition that Cowell's Directors would manage the firm for the next five years. Smith continued as Chairman and Hanson as Managing Director. By the end of 1970 both had retired and the family connection was ended. There was a period when there was a management buy back, the company largely staying afloat with 'security' work – driving licences, passports, Building Society books and the like – and a short period where there was a tie-up with Trivial Pursuits, but by the late 80s the book and colour printing was closed down and the factory sold.

A number of factors contributed to Cowell's demise as a fine colour book printer. Increased mechanisation led to Cowells losing out on their 'unique selling point' of retouching and finishing; and their stress on quality meant they could not compete on price or speed, particularly when competition from the Far East increased. Also, the very feature that made them so good to work for, and made their work force so loyal – the family atmosphere – was perhaps a shade too cosy; nepotism, at all levels, should have given way to objective selection and management development. But perhaps key to the running down was the retirement of Smith and Hanson, and eventually Scott; gone was the evangelism and energy of the trio who had been responsible for Cowell's 'halcyon' days.

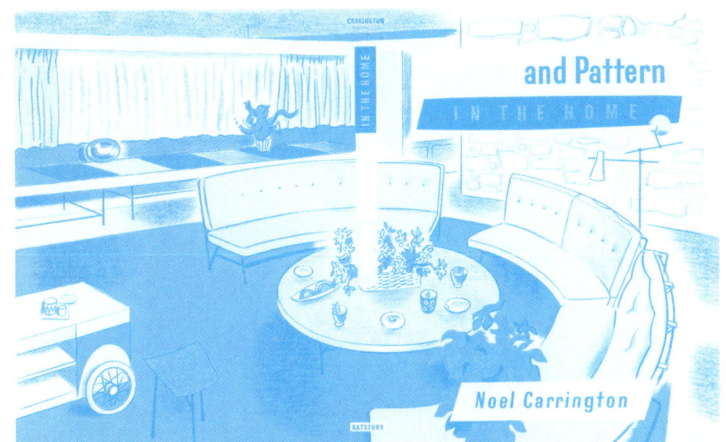

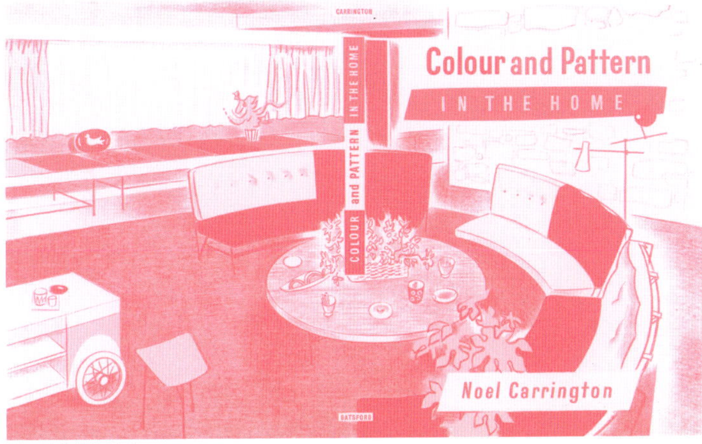

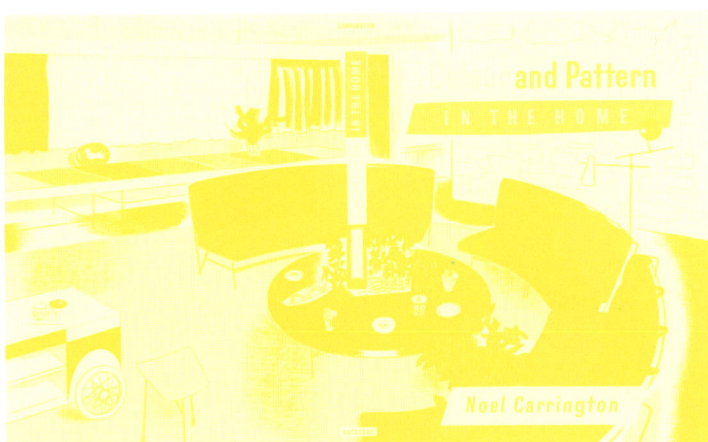

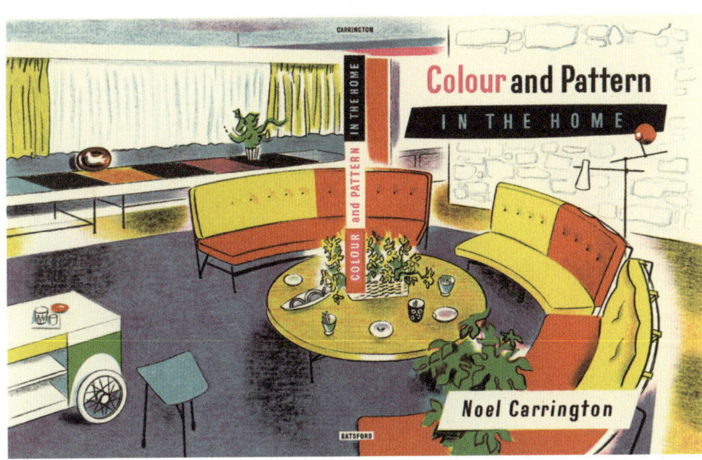

Progressive proofs for Colour and Pattern in the Home – *designed by Roland Collins*

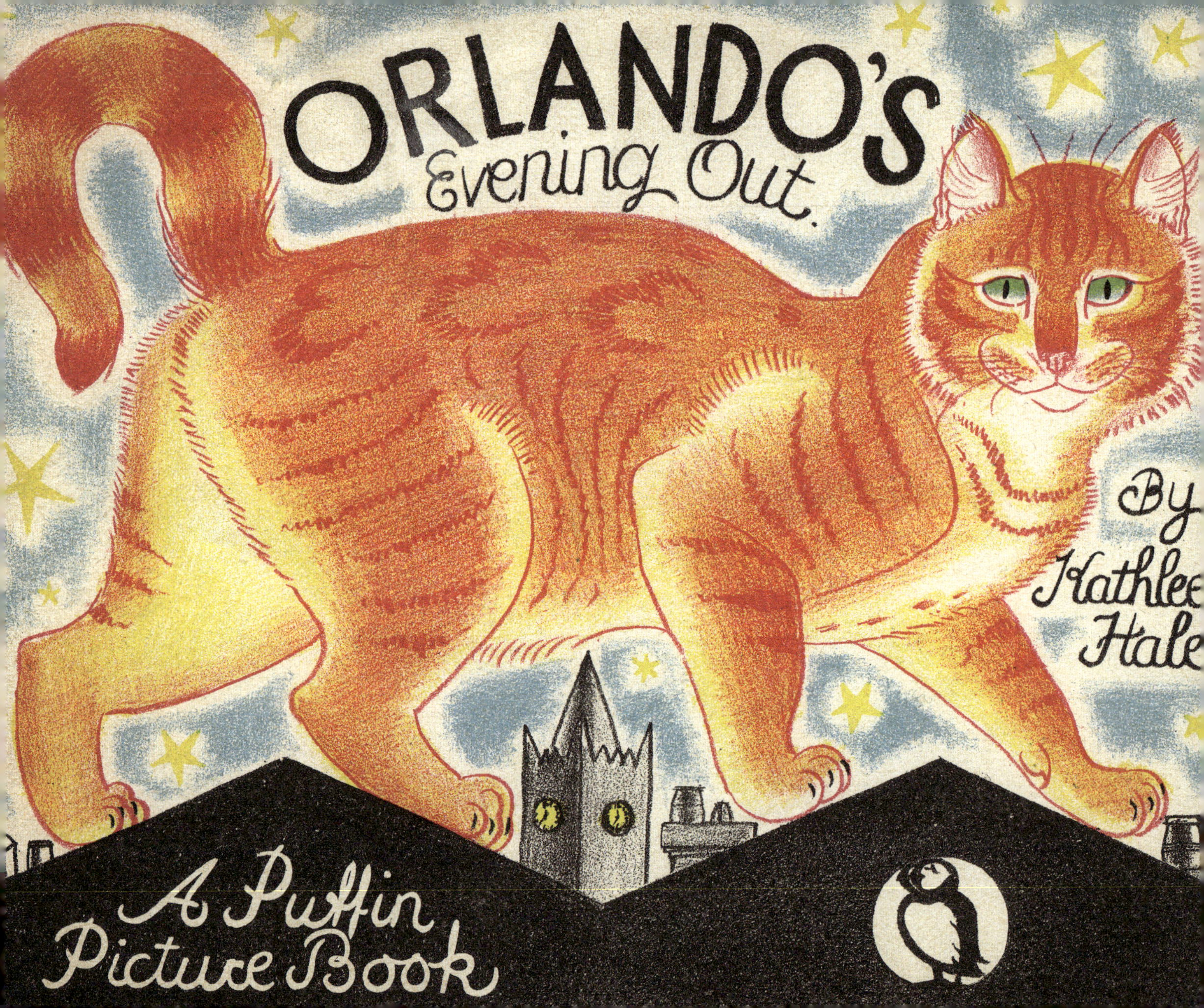
ORLANDO'S
Evening Out.
By
Kathlee
Hale
A Puffin
Picture Book

Part Two

ILLUSTRATED BOOK WORKS

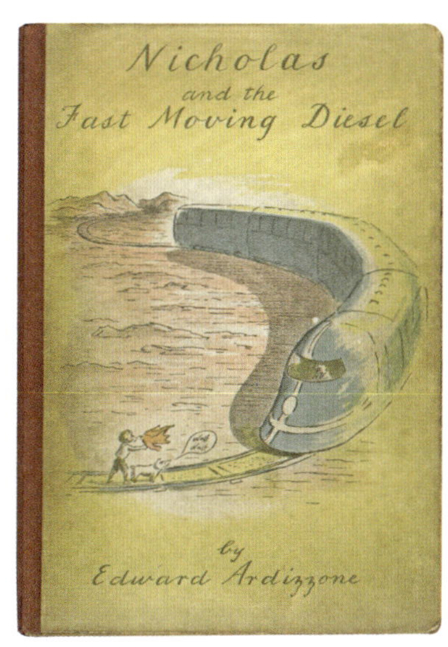

Babar the Elephant, 1934

Ardizzone and the Little Tim Books, 1937

Kathleen Hale and Orlando, the Marmalade Cat, 1938

The Puffin Picture Books, from 1940

Ravilious and Submarine Dream, 1940/1941

John Lewis and A Handbook of Printing Type, 1948

The School Prints, 1948

The Aldeburgh Festival Programme, 1948

The Royal Philatelic Collection, 1952

The Place of Crowning, 1953

David Gentleman and the Limited Editions Club, 1963

Wild Flowers of The United States, 1966

Chalk Magazine, 1970/1971

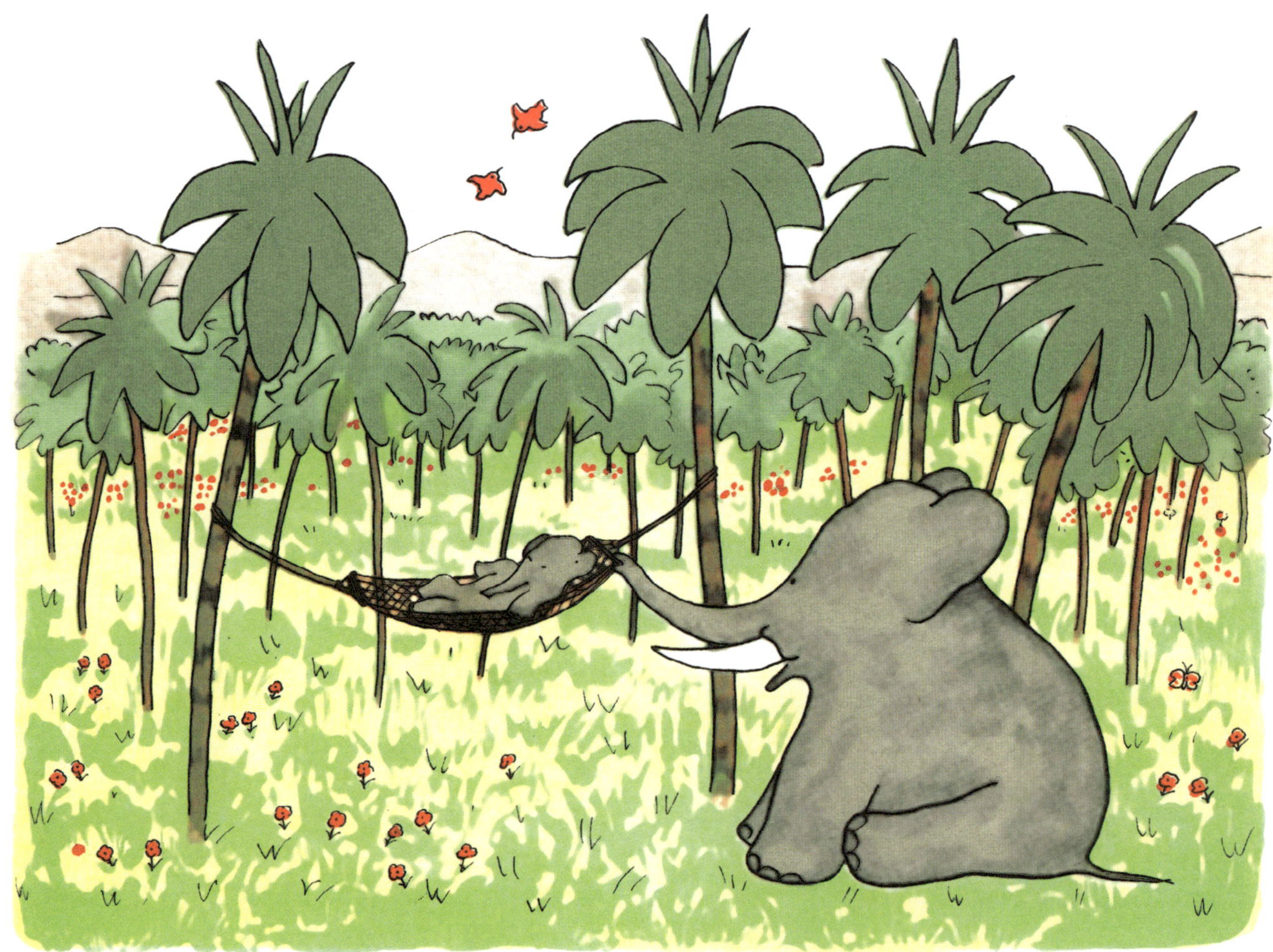

Illustrations from The Story of Babar *by Jean de Brunhoff, 1934*

1934

BABAR THE ELEPHANT

The *Babar the Elephant* books, written and illustrated by Jean de Brunhoff, and published by Hachette, were an instant success in France; and soon publishers in England and America were eager to get translations onto the market. A.A. Milne, in his introduction to the first UK translation wrote:

> 'Two years ago at a friend's house I was introduced to Babar and Celeste. They spoke French then and they spoke it with a charming simplicity which saved me from all embarrassment. With a little trouble I managed to get them into my house; and with no trouble at all they settled down at once as part of the family. Since then I have been insisting that my publishers should take out naturalisation papers for them, and let them settle down in everybody else's family.'

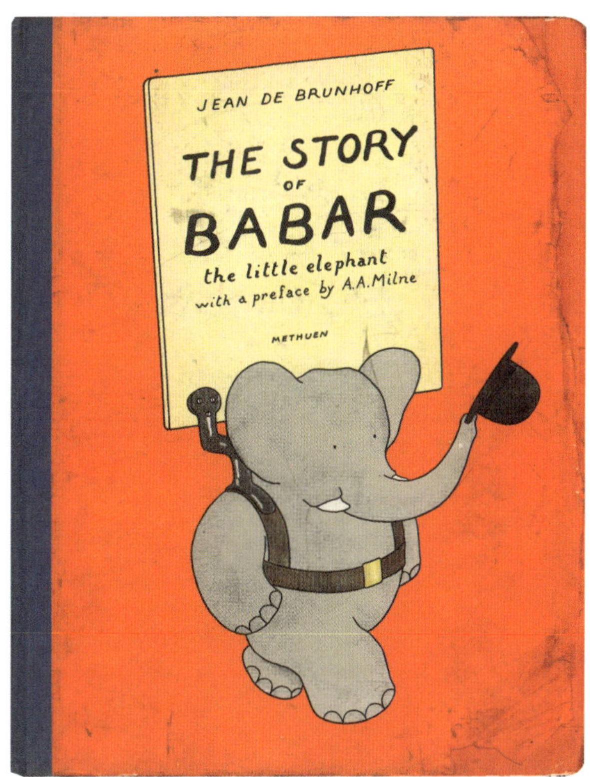

First English edition of The Story of Babar *by Jean de Brunhoff, printed by W.S. Cowell Ltd., 1934*

Whether Milne was actually instrumental in persuading Methuen to take up *Babar* is not recorded, but they did, in fact, obtain the UK rights for the series. They proceeded to look for a printer capable of handling the considerable technical challenges of reproducing the wonderfully vibrant colour images.

There were, perhaps, no more than half a dozen British printers at that time able to carry out such an assignment, including the Curwen Press, the Baynard Press and Chromoworks. But it was to Cowells that Methuen turned and Cowells indeed found the

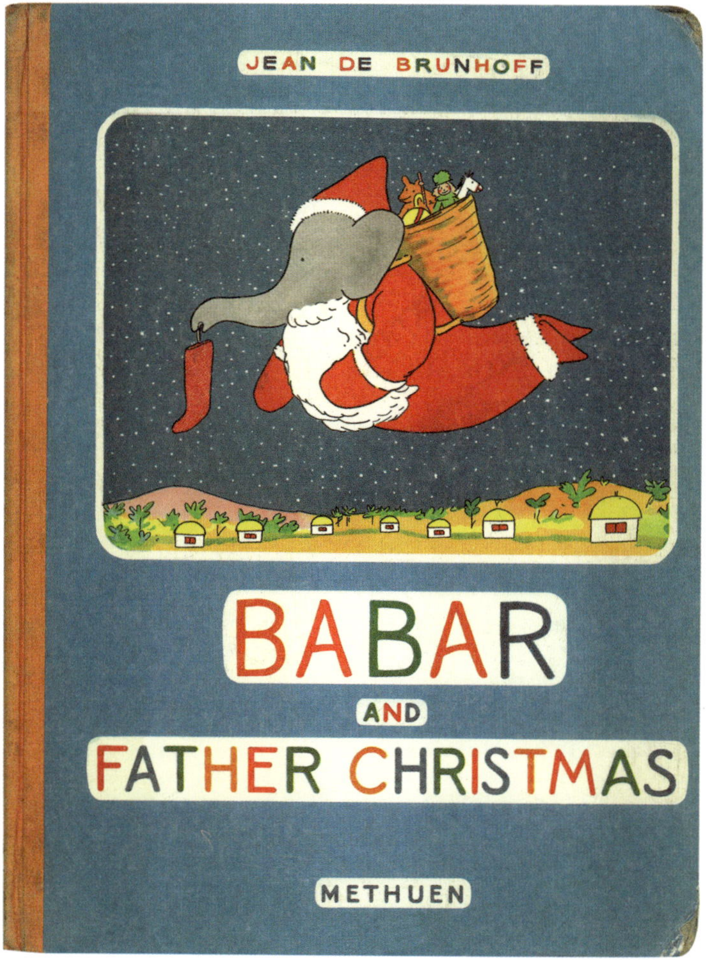

JEAN DE BRUNHOFF

BABAR AND FATHER CHRISTMAS

METHUEN

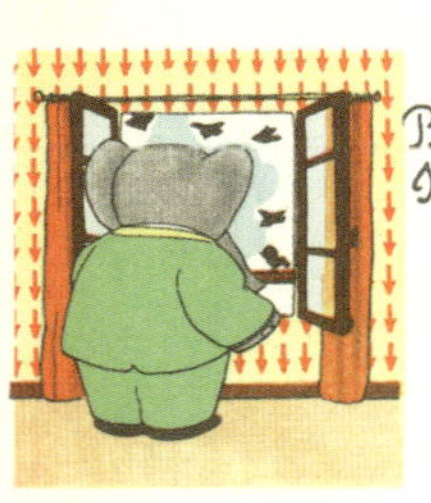

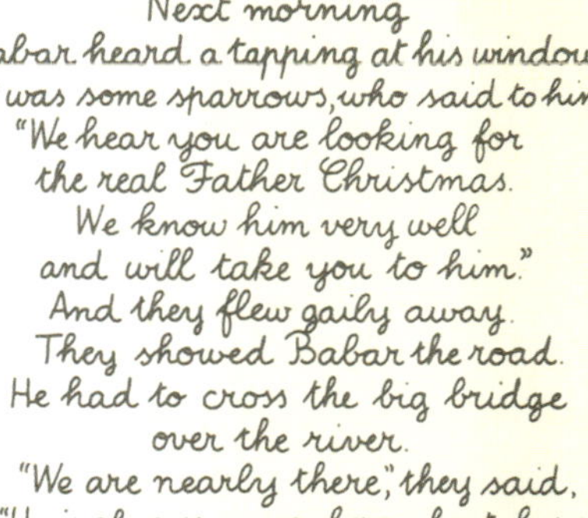

Next morning
Babar heard a tapping at his window.
It was some sparrows, who said to him:
"We hear you are looking for
the real Father Christmas.
We know him very well
and will take you to him."
And they flew gaily away.
They showed Babar the road.
He had to cross the big bridge
over the river.
"We are nearly there," they said,
"He is always somewhere about here.
Usually he sleeps under the bridges."
"Goodness! How funny!" thought Babar.
"There he is! There he is!"
cried the little birds altogether.
"He is over there

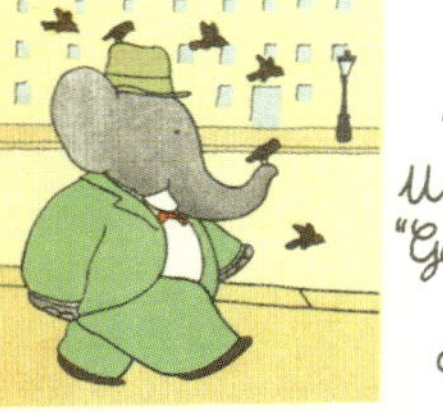

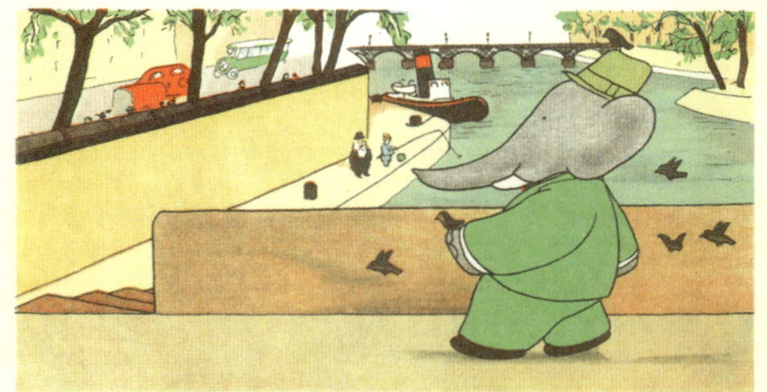

14

Babar and Father Christmas *by Jean de Brunhoff*

work something of a challenge. Their litho manager would make trips to Paris in order to bring back the litho pulls personally, to ensure that they had not dried out before being put down on the plates at Ipswich.

Both the author and the publisher expressed delight with the proofs and the latter wrote to Smith:

> 'Now all that remains is for us BOTH to make some money from the series.'

Cowells went on to print subsequent books in the series and would obviously have hoped to gain thereby; but of greater importance to the company was that Smith had been bitten by the bug of printing books, particularly coloured books for children.

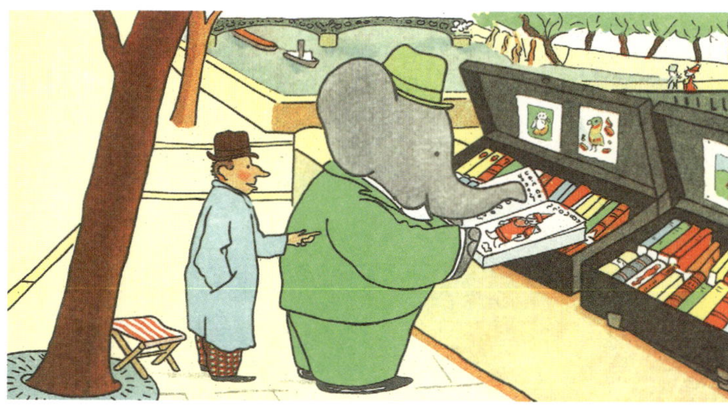

Babar and Father Christmas *(above)*
The Story of Babar *(right)*
Both illustrated by Jean de Brunhoff

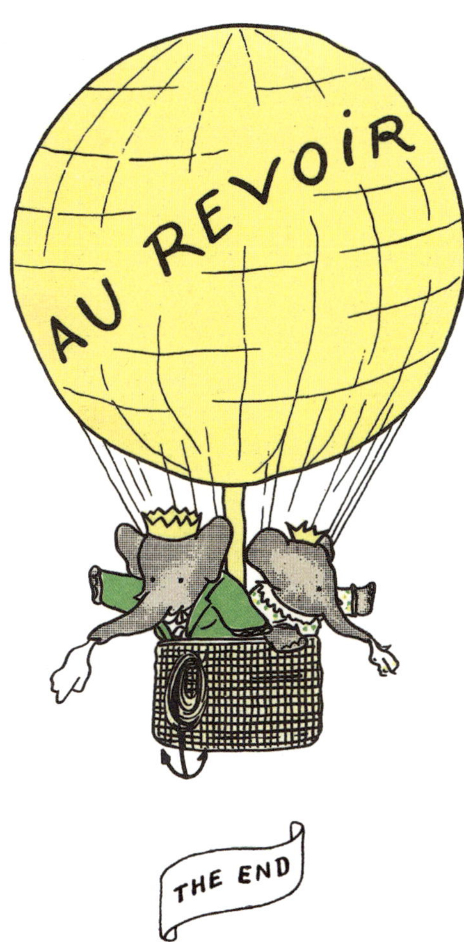

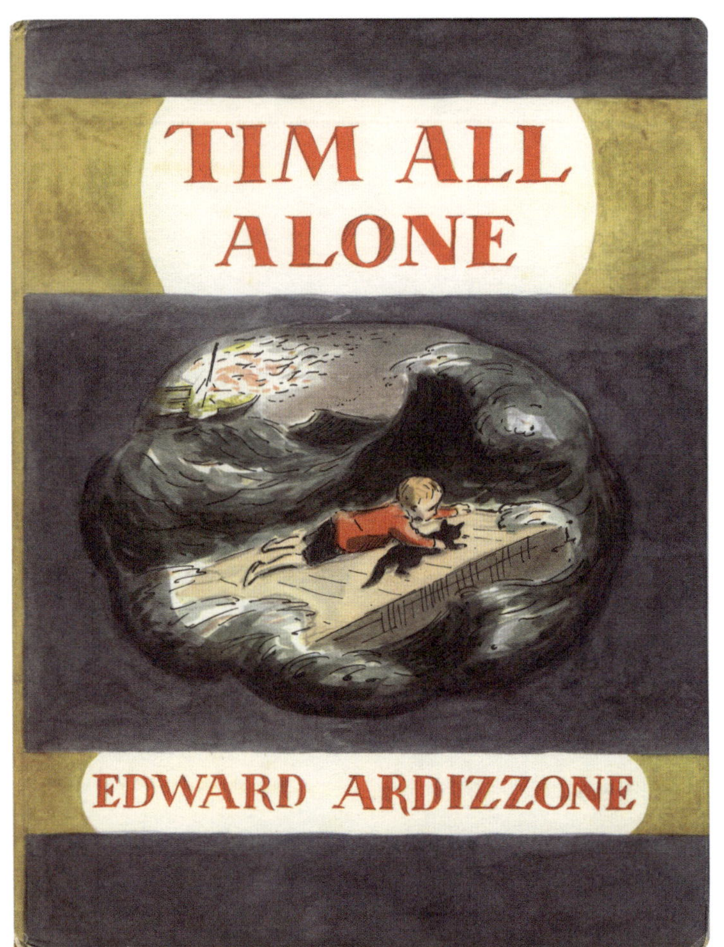

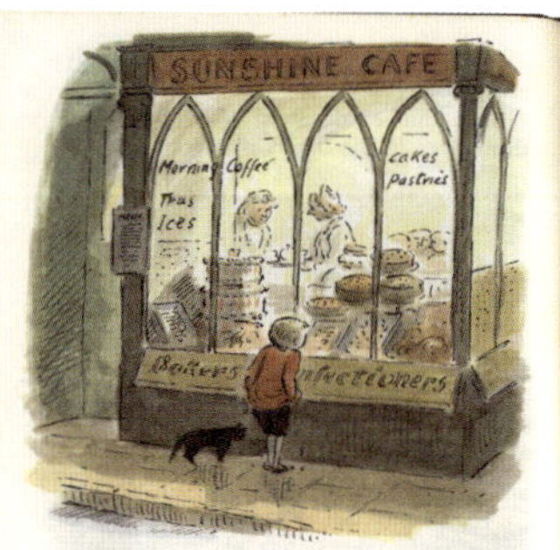

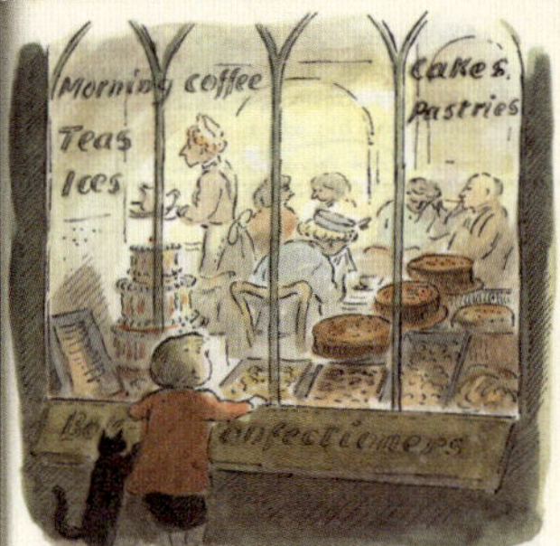

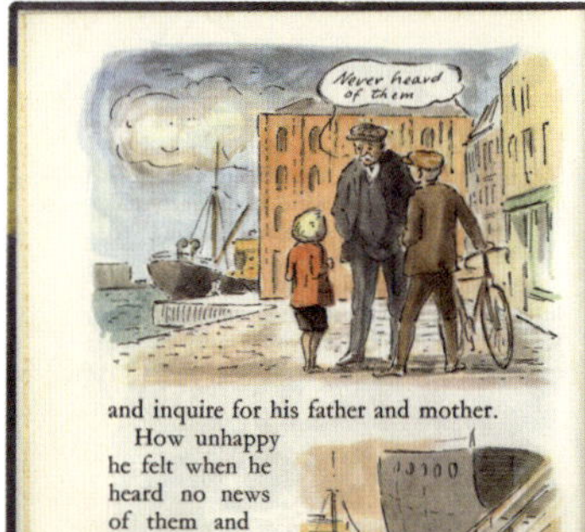

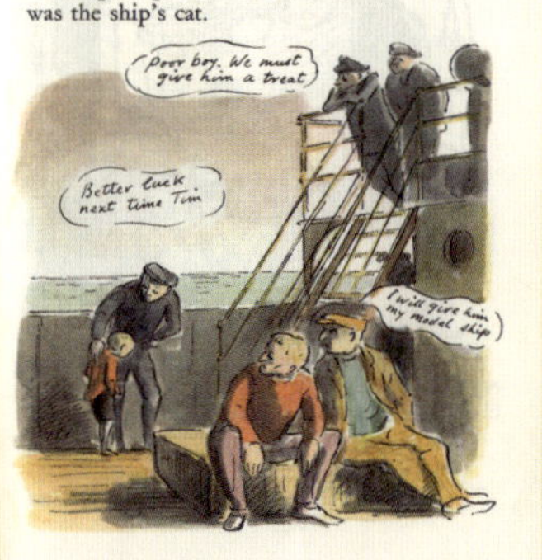

Tim All Alone, *1958*

1937

ARDIZZONE AND THE LITTLE TIM BOOKS

Edward Ardizzone was one of the most prolific book illustrators in Britain, mid-20th century. He was to illustrate and/or provide book jackets for several hundred titles, including a number he wrote himself. Tracing the printers with whom he worked is a tortuous business, with many of the books, and their reprints, being placed with different publishers, and consequently different printers.

What is established is that he worked with Cowells in 1937 with *Lucy Brown and Mr. Grimes*; and the Ardizzone family were still with Cowells in 1973, with Aingelda Ardizzone's *The Night Ride*. In all some dozen Ardizzone illustrated books were printed at Ipswich including some commercial oddities as Guinness's *Game Pie* and Shell's *Land*. It is perhaps indicative of Ardizzone's confidence in Cowells that he placed his autobiographical sketch *The Young Ardizzone* with them, in 1970.

Ardizzone's *Little Tim* books were initially devised to amuse his son Philip. Ardizzone had spent some of his childhood in Ipswich with his grandmother, whilst his father was working abroad, (1909-1912). He is said to have nurtured an early interest in the shipping coming in and out of the port, particularly in the little coasters. It was these memories, along with visits to his brother, at one time living near Deal, that became source material for his books.

The first *Little Tim* book – *Little Tim and the Brave Sea Captain* – was curiously printed in America as the manuscript, by chance, happened to land on the desk of Geoffrey Chambers, then responsible for Oxford University Press's interests there.

It was Ardizzone's next children's book – *Lucy Brown and Mr. Grimes,* that was printed at Cowells in 1937 as was the subsequent volume in the series – *Tim and Lucy go to Sea* in 1938. In all, Cowells were involved in at least one edition of all the *Little Tim* books, including the redrawn 1955 edition of *Little Tim and the Brave Sea Captain.*

For the first three of the series Ardizzone hand-coloured his drawings, but for the later ones he made colour separations on plastic sheets that Cowells were experimenting with at the time, thus reducing the cost to both publisher and printer by reducing the need for expensive photographic work. He sketched out his working methods in an article he wrote for the *Penrose Annual* (1952). In this he described his delight in working in line and wash by 'combining the beauty of swift flowing line with clear soft colours', but appreciated its drawback of being expensive to reproduce. His experiments with transparent plastic sheets, separating the pen and ink outlines from the colour washes, came to satisfy both his publishers, Oxford University Press, and Cowells, and he was to use the method for the rest of his work there. He wrote of his relationship with the Cowell's operatives:

> '...if the artist can collaborate with the printers and plate makers as I did over my last book *Tim and Charlotte* the

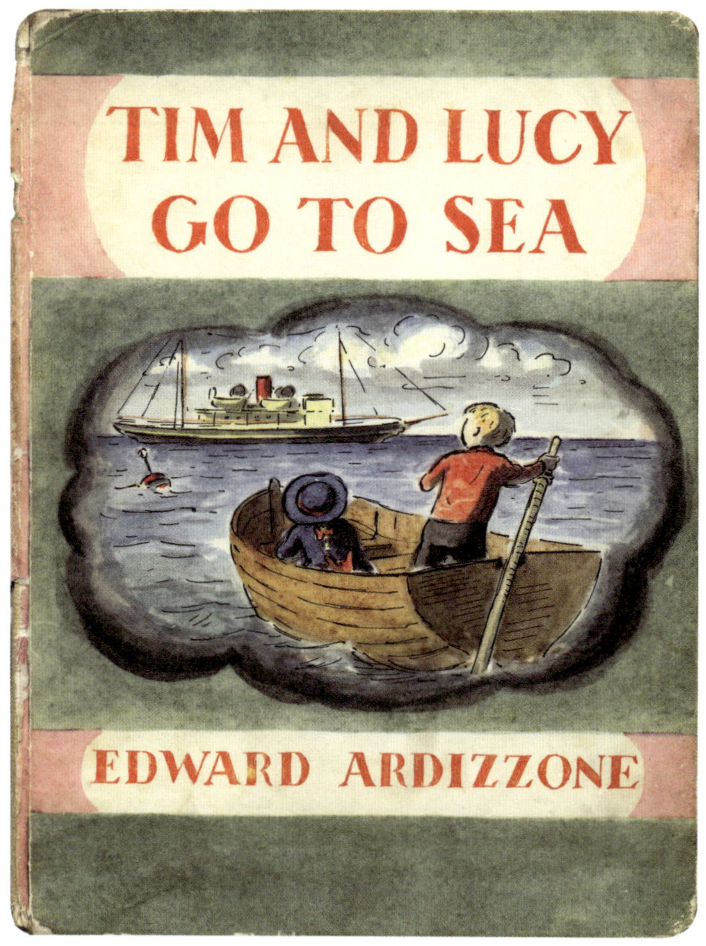

Tim and Lucy Go To Sea, *1960*

result can be a delightful interpretation of the original colour, and something far more pleasing to look at than the bad approximation achieved by the usual methods.'

There is definitely a strong line to be put under Ardizzone's 'if', for his illustrations tended to be rather delicately coloured, resulting in somewhat smoky proofs. Cowells printers would tend to strengthen the colours in order to clarify the images and this was not to Ardizzone's taste. Rarely did any of the proofs pass first inspection and were only signed off when a sufficient lightening had taken place.

John Lewis, who overlapped with Ardizzone when he was working with Cowells, thought the eventual images were delightfully fresh. Certainly *Little Tim* pleased the children of the time, and, even now, a third generation on, the books are not only still popular but have a cult following with collectors of children's literature.

Ardizzone's work with Cowells strengthened their reputation, particularly for coloured children's books, and Cowell's pride in their 'Ardizzone connection' lingered on in those who had worked on his books, long after the company's demise. When a new footbridge was being built in Ipswich and suggestions for naming it were sought, Ardizzone's was one put forward; and there is still a campaign to get a blue plaque to him for at least one of his grandparents' houses in which he had stayed as a boy.

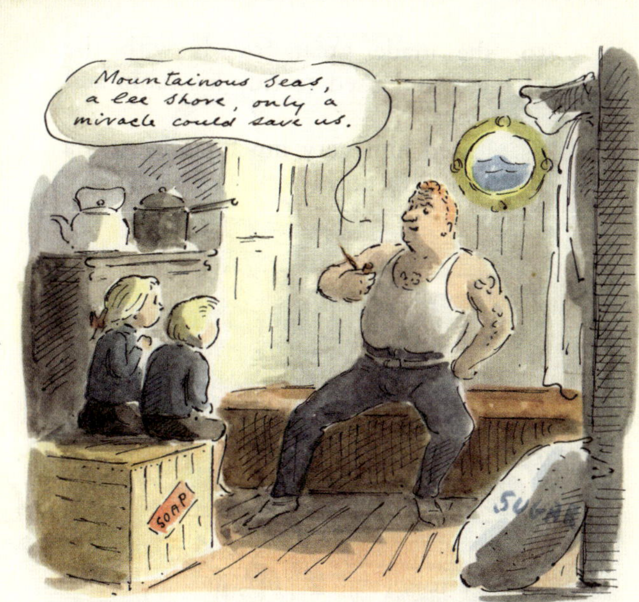

Often Tim and Lucy would go to the galley. If the cook was busy they would help him with the cooking, but if he was free, he would sit down and tell them wonderful stories of his life at sea.

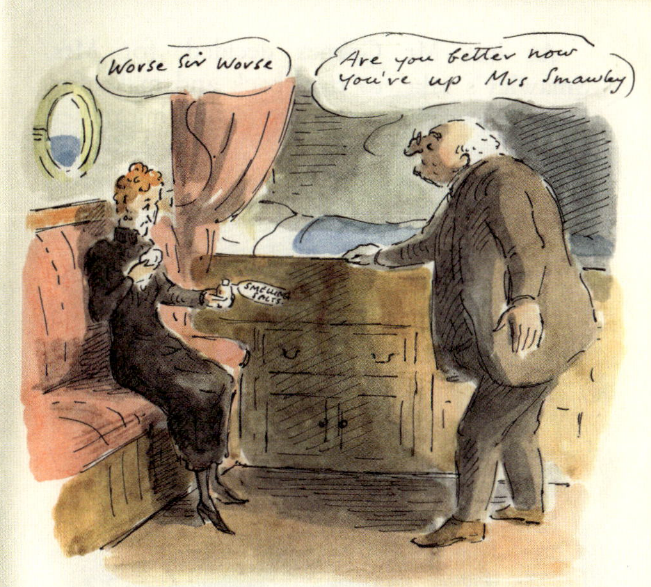

Mr Grimes was happy too, but Mrs Smawley became sadder and sadder and more and more sick, until Mr Grimes felt he had been unkind to make her come to sea with him.

Tim and Lucy Go To Sea, *1960*

1938

KATHLEEN HALE AND ORLANDO, THE MARMALADE CAT

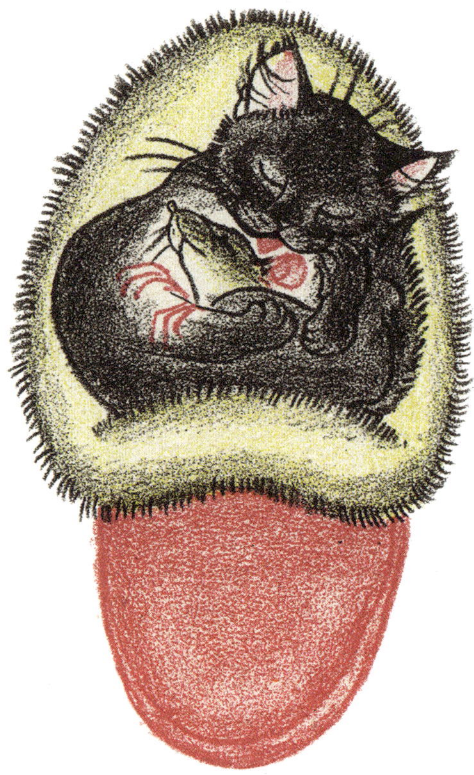

Illustration from Orlando's Home Life

Kathleen Hale could be said to have had a disturbed childhood leading on to a rather rackety life as a young woman. Being an artist was always a thread in her motivation, sometimes a rather tenuous one, and two years at Reading University Art Department helped little. Leaving Didsbury for London she soon found herself drawn into artistic circles – friendship with the Epsteins, visits to the Studio Club and the Cave of Harmony, a period as Augustus John's secretary and life in Fitzrovia, which was at its most Bohemian just prior to, and after World War One.

Odd design commissions turned up – some book jackets for W.H. Smith, a mural at the Wembley Exhibition Centre, and occasional sales of her own art work. Eventually, however, she married a doctor, lived in the Home Counties, brought up two sons, and became a country doctor's wife.

Amongst the family's animals was a small marmalade cat which they had named Orlando after a small ginger-headed child they had come across at a Tuscan railway station! Finding a dearth of children's books to read to her sons, Hale started making up stories about Orlando, and, on a friend's suggestion, began making them up into books – doing both text and illustrations. Orlando was given the kind of family Hale had missed, and a variety of her Fitzrovian friends got woven into the plots. Orlando himself was given qualities Hale felt were characteristic of her doctor husband – wisdom, reliability and kindness.

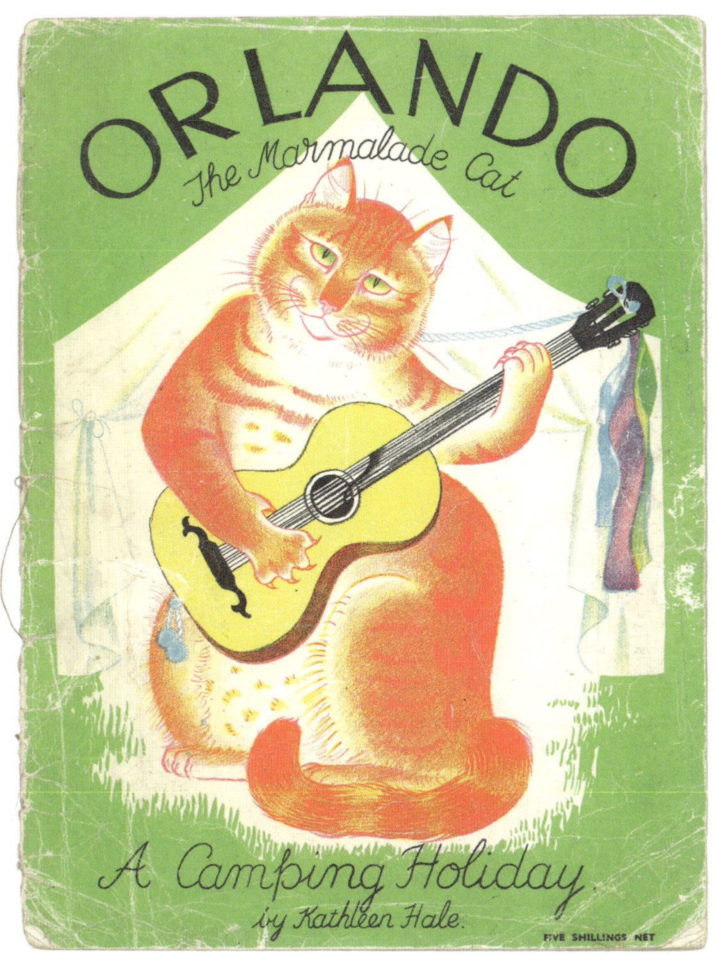

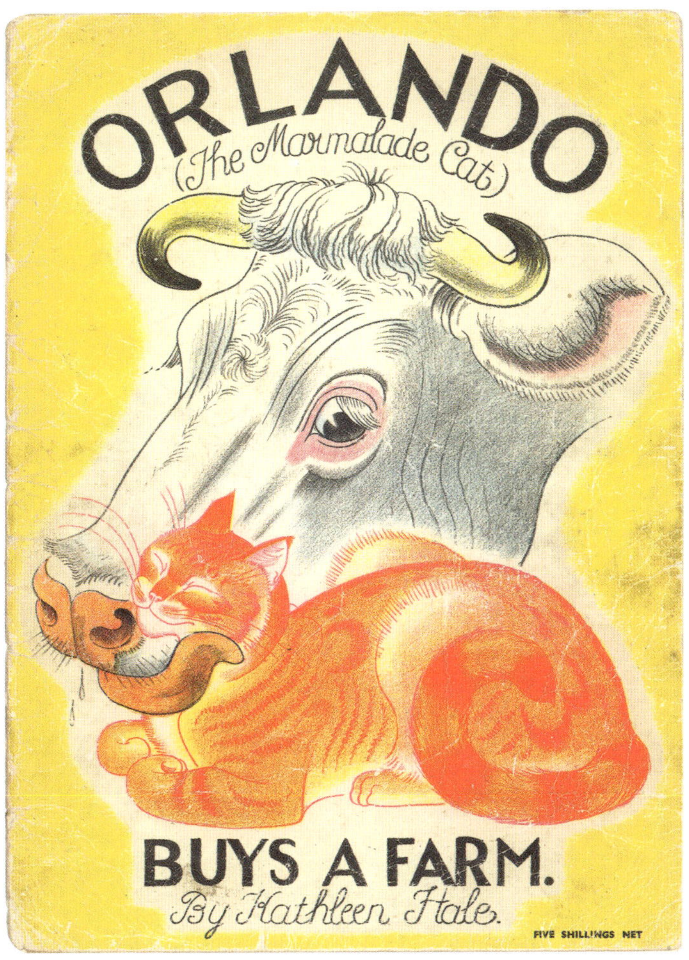

Orlando, the Marmalade Cat *book covers*

Hale put her first two books – *Orlando's Camping Holiday* and *Orlando's Trip Abroad* – to a literary agent, with no success. It is not clear how she knew Geoffrey Smith, but she described him as a friend, and as 'running a small printing firm cum wine merchants, whose work consisted of advertisements, trade cards and the like'! Luckily for Hale, Smith was keen to develop the quality books side of the business, having already the experience of *Babar*, and perhaps saw Hale's frustrations as his opportunity.

Armed with the two *Orlando* roughs, Smith went to see Noel Carrington, then an editor at *Country Life*, who was taking an interest in auto-lithographed children's books at the time. The *Orlando* books met the needs of all three – Hale to resurrect her creative career, Carrington to test out his ideas on publishing cheap illustrated children's books, and Smith to break out beyond the bounds of run-of-the-mill commercial printing. Serendipity! Of her first meeting with Carrington, Hale wrote:

> 'I walked out of *Country Life's* Covent Garden offices – past the church porch where I had slept on sacks at dawn as a land girl – in a state of utter bliss. I was an Author.'

Hale was all about having largeness and colour, but Carrington, from his work at *Country Life*, was all too aware of cost. Smith came to the rescue by demonstrating how Hale's extravagant colour range could be reduced to four plates – red, yellow, blue and black – with some over-printing. Carrington was persuaded, and the two *Orlando* books were published by *Country Life* and printed at Cowells.

Orlando's Camping Holiday was lithographed by Cowell's artists, from Hale's illustrations; but the expense of this (the detailed work

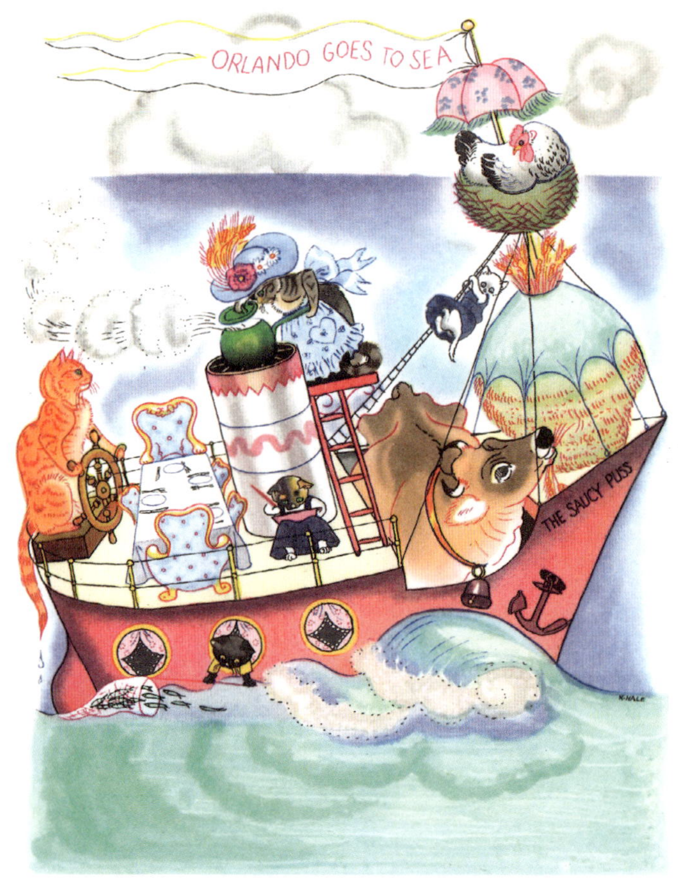

Orlando Goes to Sea, *1956*

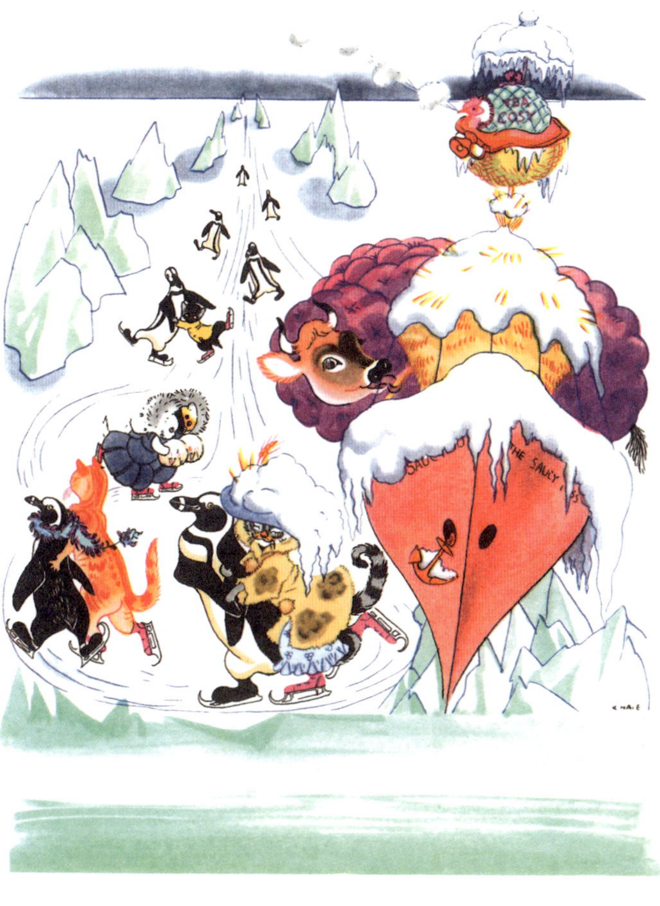

Orlando Goes to Sea, *1956*

with every rabbit, snail, beetle, etc.) led to Hale volunteering to do the lithography herself. Smith arranged for her to do this at the Works, and, whereas the printers could well have been resentful or even have 'downed tools' at this, Hale found them ready to go out of their way to help her – 'particularly Mr. Patrick and Mr. Fenner.'

Her artistic exuberance could have alarmed them when, as skilled artisans, they were determined to examine patiently every chalk line she made to ensure that the spread of grains was exactly right for the colour desired; but as a working relationship was established that suited all parties Hale reported the results as 'surprisingly good'. There was the small matter of Hale not being a fully paid up union member, but when it was discovered that the union would not accept women, the matter was quietly dropped.

Once Hale had experimented with the zinc plates to get the surface roughened sufficiently for the effect she wanted, she decided to work at home. The unwieldly plates (each large enough to carry four pages) had to be crated at Ipswich and sent by rail, and returned by the same means. With Cowell's development of the lightweight plastic sheets which they now called Plastowcowell, the whole process was eased. Once completed, the plastic sheets were photographed on to metal ones, which were then inked with the appropriate colours and printed.

Cowells had produced a special drawing board for Plastocowell – a tilted wooden frame enclosing a large panel of Perspex. When a bulb was placed under the frame the light would shine up through the Perspex, illuminating the plastic plate lying on it. Each plate had registration marks and margins marked out at Cowells to ensure exact registration when the colours were being overprinted, and this was further aided by the two holes on each plate which went over studs on the frame to avoid plate movement. Hale was happy with this contraption as it meant she was now able 'to get the black of Orlando's eyes in the right place and not on his nose.'

In spite of supportive printers Hale nevertheless still found the whole process of auto-lithography nerve-racking – watching for every surplus mark or thumbprint, carrying the colour combinations in her mind, working on one hundred and twenty-eight plates for each book – let alone having to remove everything to the garden shed when the children came home from school. One book could take her up to four or five months to complete.

By the time Hale got to work on the third book, Carrington had left *Country Life* and the new editor was reluctant to take any more *Orlando's* on as they were not selling particularly well. Hale claimed that it was she who mentioned to Carrington the possibility of Penguin being interested in children's books but that he had shown no interest in the suggestion. Carrington does not record this, but, whatever the situation, he did persuade Allen Lane to the idea and Hale was asked to do another book – *Orlando's Evening Out* – which became the first Puffin Picture Book, albeit not numbered in the series, and Cowells continued to be *Orlando's* printer.

Hale was only to do one more book for the Puffin series – *Orlando's Home Life* – possibly as the series came to focus on 'knowledge' rather than 'fiction'. After World War Two she was published either by *Country Life* or *Harlequin* (John Murray's imprint which was also edited by Carrington). That *Orlando* was published at all, and was to become so popular, was due, to a considerable extent, to Smith's imaginative support and to the tolerance, patience and skill of his lithographic artists and printers.

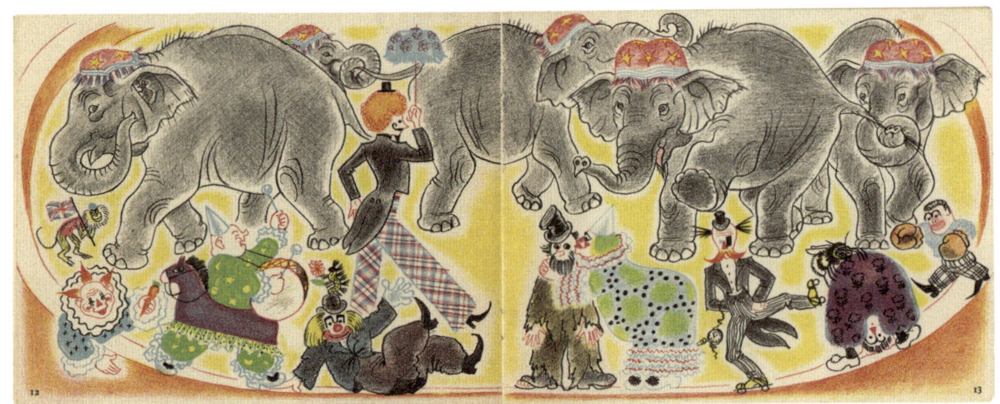

Orlando's Evening Out

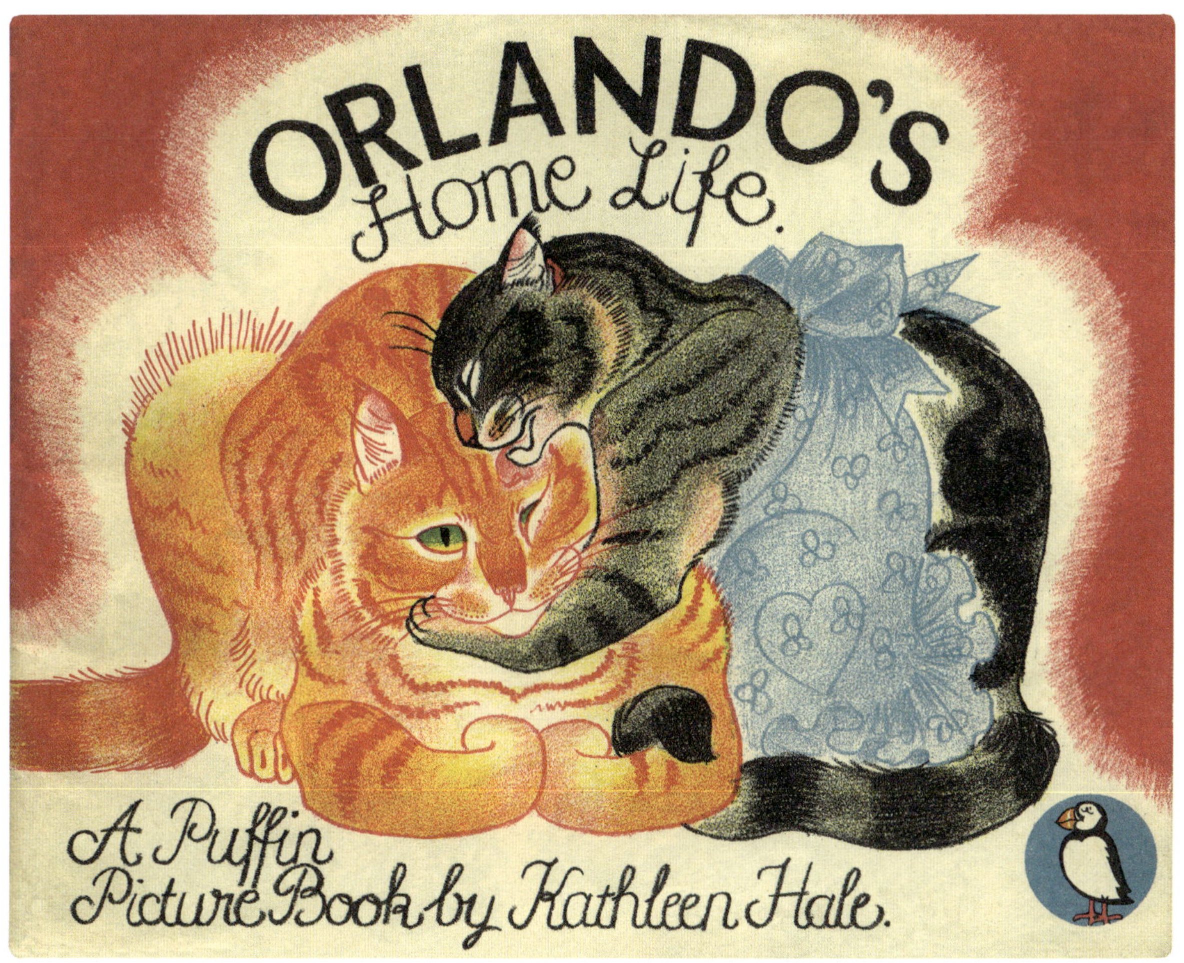

Orlando's Home Life

From 1940

THE PUFFIN PICTURE BOOKS

When Geoffrey Smith decided to take Cowells into illustrated book production he could have had little idea of the problems that arose with Penguin, and its commissioned artists and authors, for the Puffin Picture Books.

Noel Carrington, already well-known as an editor in the 1930s, finding a dearth of 'factual' children's books to feed the inquisitive minds of his own children, began to explore the possibility of filling the market gap. He had come across the *Pere Castor* series of French illustrated children's books, one of which had just been published in English translation by Allen & Unwin. At about the same time, Pearl Binder had just returned from one of her reportage visits to the Soviet Union with some coloured children's books that had been extremely cheaply produced. And, as if by zeitgeist, Harold Curwen showed Carrington some of Barnett Freedman's remarkable coloured auto-lithography at much the same time as Smith had already convinced Carrington about lithography with the *Orlando* books.

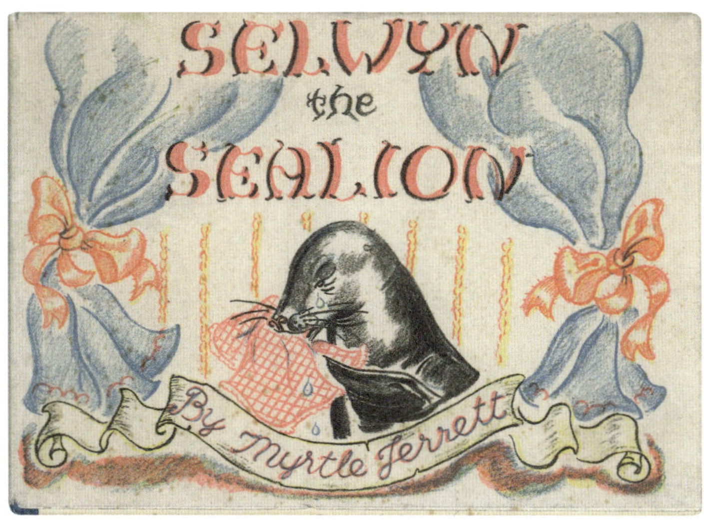

Selwyn the Sealion, *illustrated by Myrtle Jerret, published by Noel Carrington at Country Life Limited, 1948*

Carrington's ideas for children's 'knowledge' books in colour lithography became a reality with his chance meeting at a Double Crown Club dinner, in 1938, with Allen Lane. Lane had, just two years previously, launched Penguin Books, his 'democratisation' of reading. Although Lane did not immediately react to Carrington's suggestions for extending Penguin Books to children's reading, on his return from a trip to India he contacted Carrington and

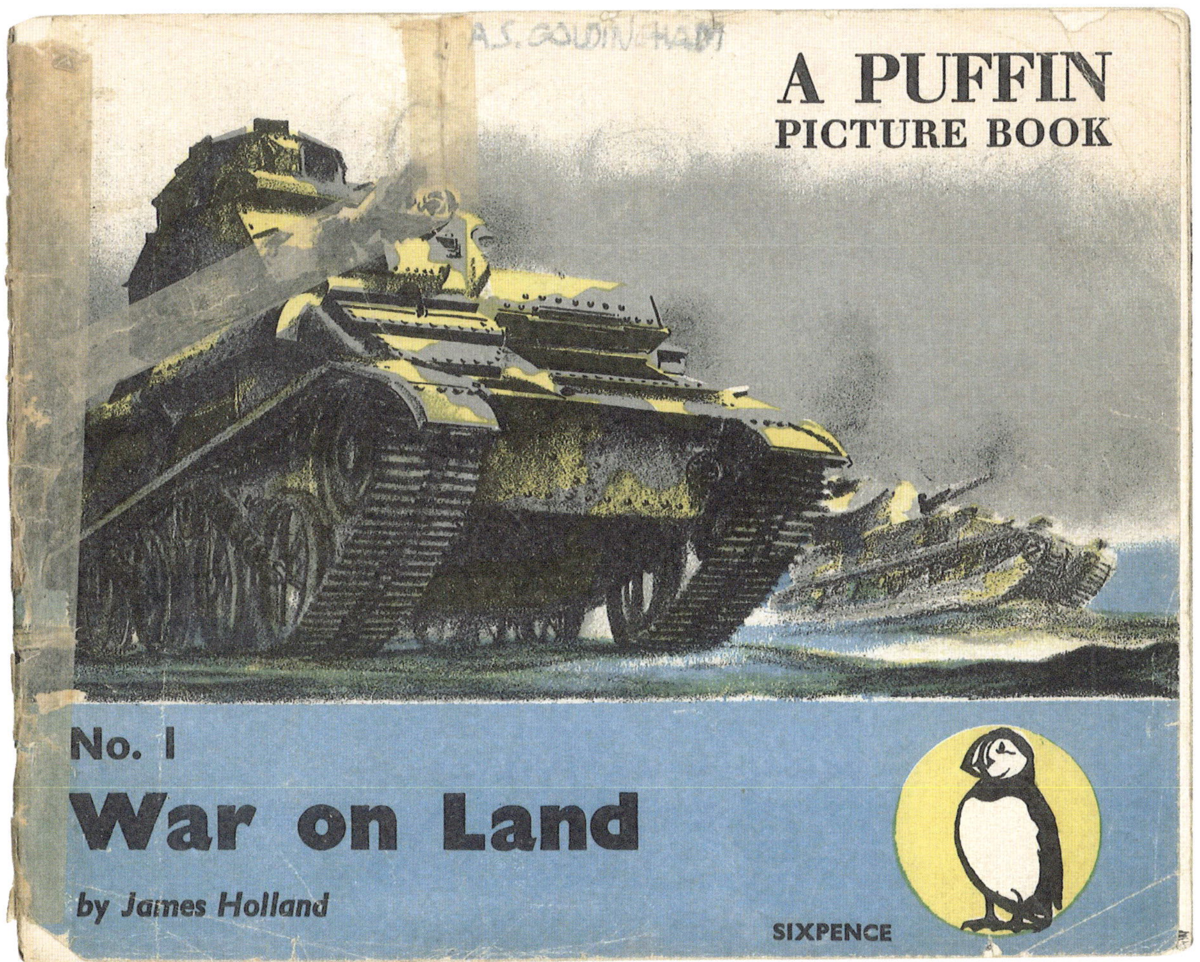

War on Land, *1940*

commissioned him to edit and produce what became the Puffin Picture Books. The time seemed just right, to Lane, with wartime evacuation plans afoot, that not only would there be a shortage of children's books available cheaply in rural areas, but that evacuee town children would need to be educated in country ways.

Meanwhile Carrington had already involved Cowells by asking Smith to carry out a feasibility study of the possibility of producing children's books cheaply. Carrington wrote of Smith's contribution (*Penrose Annual* 1957):

> 'If the enterprise came to be associated with hand-drawn lithography it was because Geoffrey Smith convinced me that only thus could initial costs be kept sufficiently low to be sold at sixpence.' (Sixpence being the going rate of Penguins at that time.)

To Cowells the scheme was to provide a godsend (as well as a headache) to help keep them afloat during the war. Cowells worked with Carrington to produce the first five Puffin Picture Books, and some twenty were printed there during the war. Smith was enthusiastic about the work for it brought him the desired contact with artists and authors, as well as contributing to Cowell's growing reputation for bookwork.

The production of each title tended to start with a honeymoon period, with optimism of the fresh partnership to be involved. Typically enthusiastic were the husband and wife team, Alexander and Margaret Potter, new to the lithographic process, writing to Carrington of their visit to Ipswich to start on their *A History of the Countryside* (29th November 1943):

> 'We had a most enjoyable time at Ipswich, and Mr. Geoffrey Smith was indeed a charming host. Everybody there was most eager to be of assistance to us, and we have learned a great deal.'

However, reality soon set in for Smith, and the warmth and excitement with which each title was started, as with some marriages, soon became cooler and more restrained, when the partners actually had to 'live' together over a period of time, and cope with the practical realities of book making. There is unavoidable conflict when people come together for any project, ostensibly having a common aim, yet each party actually having their own personal agenda and schedule, let alone size of ego.

For Cowells, besides increasing their income and reputation, their main concern was to achieve smooth uninterrupted runs, with minimal machine breakdowns or periods of idleness, and no undue interference from artist, author or publisher. Artists too hoped to enhance their reputations but defended their 'art' and were determined to have it reproduced to their wishes whatever the cost in delayed printing. And Penguin, besides keeping a strict control of outgoings to ensure the profitability of the venture, wanted to strengthen the moral high ground they held in being at the fore of bringing knowledge and literature to the populace at an affordable price.

In actuality, Cowells was relatively inexperienced in large edition book publishing; artists were inexperienced in the arduous travails of auto-lithography; authors, knowledgeable in their own specialisation, were unused to making their subjects palatable to children; and Penguin found the accuracy necessary to producing

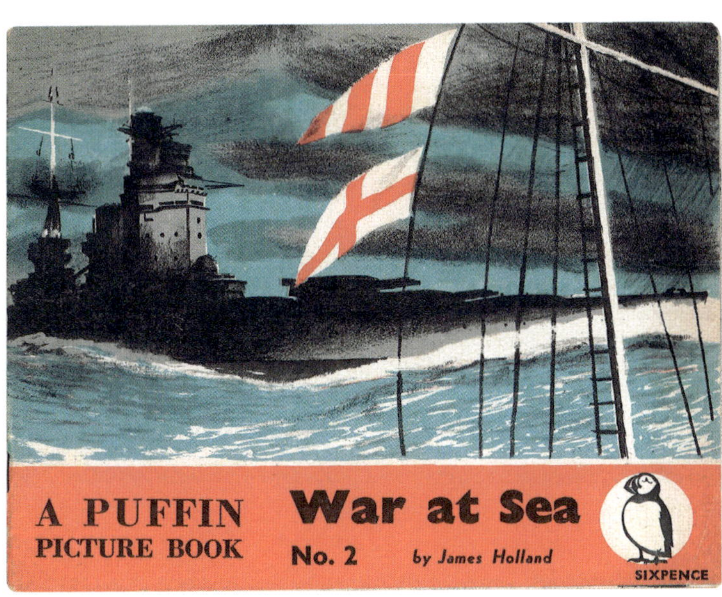

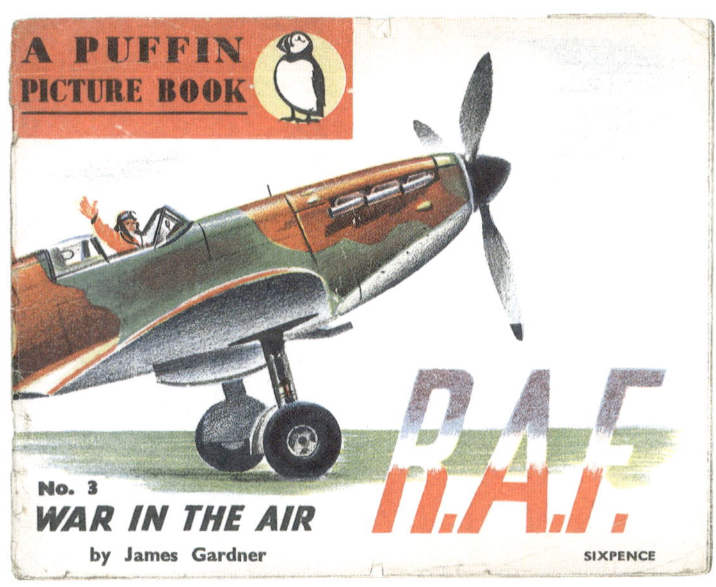

War at Sea*, 1940 (left) and* War in the Air*, 1940 (right)*

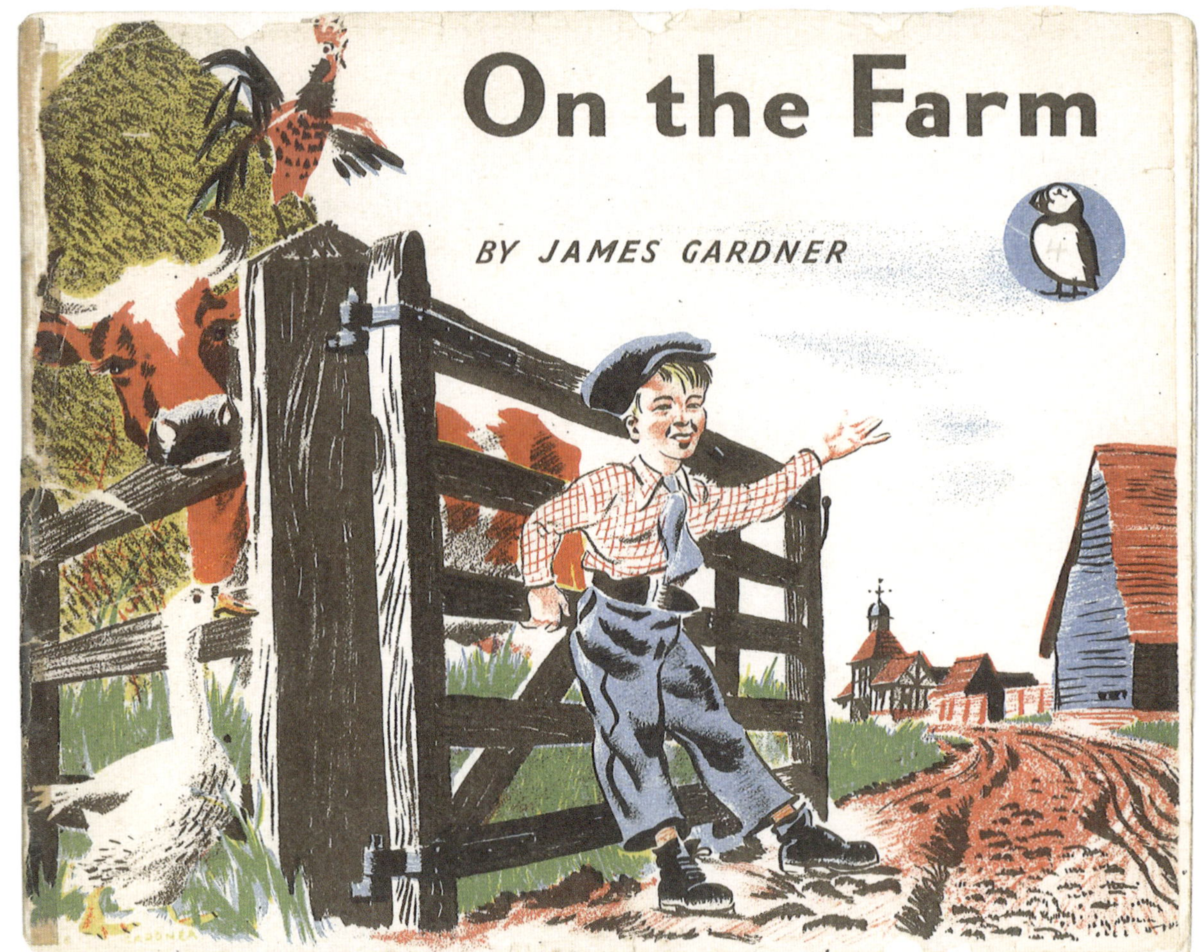

On the Farm, *1940*

technical illustrations excessively time-consuming. Any would-be publisher, illustrator, non-fiction writer or printer would find it salutary to read through the Puffin Picture Book archives (a folder for each book, the comparative bulkiness indicating the petty problems that had been involved in its production); if not completely deflected from their career ambitions, they would, at least, be forewarned of the pitfalls and frustrations to come.

Examples of unforeseen difficulties that meant re-workings or delays at Cowells, with the consequent need to renegotiate estimates, were myriad. Typical of such was specified in a letter from Carrington to James Gardner about his illustrations for *On the Farm* (10th December 1947):

> 'About the *Farm* book. I had a talk with Alfa Laval, having sent them the drawing, and they say that as 90% of the farms they supply have pail milking it would be better... This means that the little bit of pipe just over the cooler needs taking away – an easy matter I should suppose for the litho artist at Cowells...'

Progress was not smooth in the early 'rural' books of the series in that both Carrington and Lane lived in the countryside, with farming enthusiasms; nor by the fact that Lane's brother was a serious farmer. In the Potter's book – *The History of the Countryside* – for example, Lane's brother complained that 'one of the discs of the plough on the back cover is not buried in the ground as it should be...' and so the necessary changes had to be made to get the correct angle, depth, whatever, no doubt to the irritation of the artist and the printer.

Other delays occurred by writers not producing texts on time or demanding amendments when they thought the layout of their text detracted from its comprehension. Artists complained about the reproduction of colour tone (Cowell's red seems to have been particularly targeted), by inexact registration of colour, and so on. Badmin, whose *Trees in Britain* has been rated the finest volume in the series, seems to have been excessively temperamental and demanding; an unsigned note in the archives reading:

> 'Badmin does not grow less fussy as he grows older...so I only hope when he sees it he will be in one of his more mellow moods.'

The files are full of missives going to and fro between the series' 'partners', showing all possible permutations and combinations of alliances – publisher and printer v artist (for delays and amendments), printers and artist v publishers (for late contracts and delayed payments); and so on, and so on!

Of course Cowells was not without its faults and weaknesses of which one seems to have been mislaying items. Bassett-Lowke, an awkward, straight-speaking, manufacturer of models, wrote tetchily and threateningly to Carrington of *Marvellous Models and Models to Make* (3rd February 1944):

> '...I do hope your friend Smith is able to find the front cover, because it is rather expensive to redraw...'

Smith's reply, which could well have sounded alarm bells to would-be illustrators, was remarkably, irresponsibly, chirpy, along the lines

'I'm O.K., you're O.K.':

> 'I am glad to say that in this instance everybody was right and therefore everybody was happy. The missing sketch had fallen out of the parcel, and, worse than that, had fallen behind some of the steel furniture in the strong room and it was only through the observance of a 14 year old who remembered seeing the sketch sticking out that it was found at all.'

In spite of such, one hopes, not too common mishaps, many of the artists involved with the Puffin Picture Books not only learnt their lithography from Cowell's men, but looked to them for general mentoring and support such is exemplified by James Gardner's concern when he heard that his *Battle of Britain* might be printed elsewhere:

> 'I have worked before with Cowells, and there is a certain amount of handwork – laying colour tints on these sketches, I would feel much happier if the men who know the style of work were undertaking it. The touching up and laying of tints will not be done under my personal control, and I hope it will be possible to get it done by the men at Cowells who have worked with me and know the ropes and are in fact very good litho-artists – a rare thing these days.'

Cowell's standard of work, and willingness to compromise, led Penguin to retain them for some twenty-five years, from the first Puffin Picture Book – *War on Land* by James Holland published in 1940, to the last – *Seashore Life* by Gillian Matthews and Peter Parks, published in 1965. Penguin used other printers from time to time – Curwen, Harrisons, Royles, The Baynard Press, and Swains – but Cowells was the mainstay, printing over half the one hundred and twenty books in the series.

Joe Pearson, in his meticulously researched study of the Puffin Picture Books, saw Geoffrey Smith as crucial to the success of the whole project – he had made the original estimates and suggested the eventual format for the books, he had personally supervised the first four titles to ensure a sound start, he had been Cowell's liaison point with Carrington, throughout, meeting weekly with him and Lane. And when Northans of Paris showed an interest in developing the series in France it was to Cowells that Carrington turned for the large print runs of some twenty through thirty thousand.

Carrington went on to use Cowells for some of his own design books as well as those published through Transatlantic Arts; and when Chatto, heavily influenced by the Puffin Picture Books, started their own *Open Your Eyes* series of structured learning books these were to be done on Plastocowell and printed at Cowells. Cassell and Company's *Pantoscope* series, again simple learning books, not only used Cowells for their striking concertina illustrated pull out and for their covers, but were to employ some of the Puffin Picture Book artists, such as Paxton Chadwick.

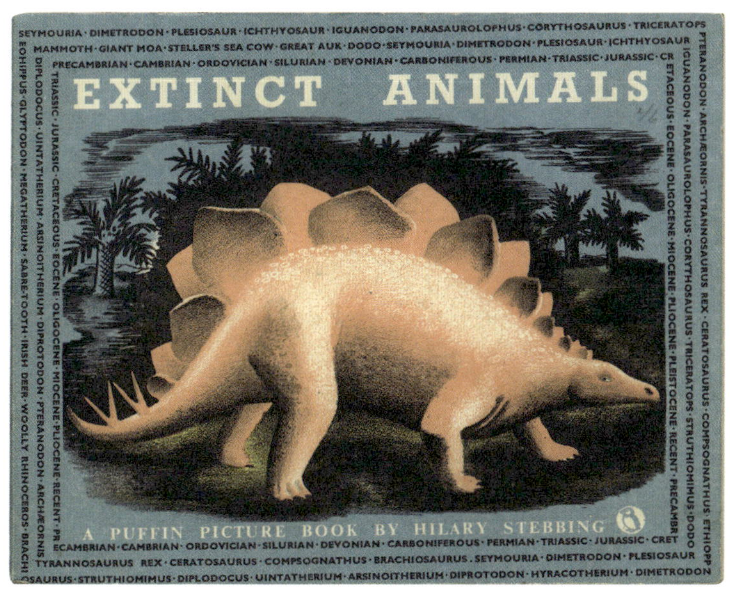

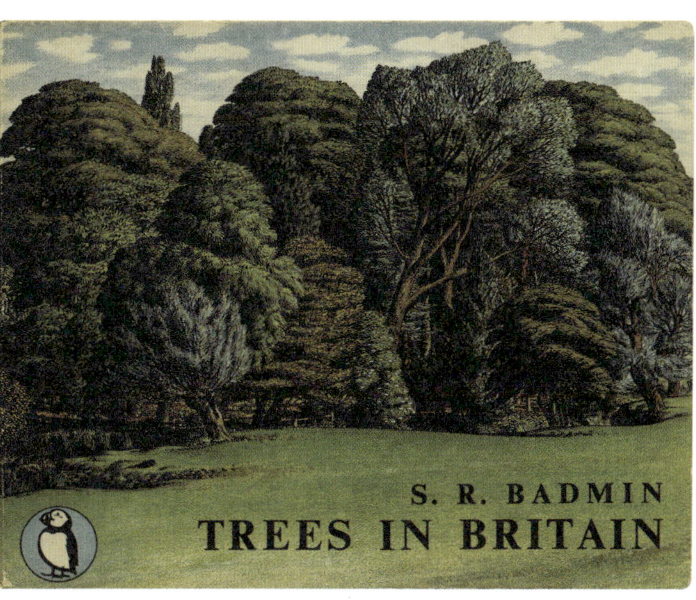

Extinct Animals, *1946 (left) and* Trees in Britain, *1957 (right)*

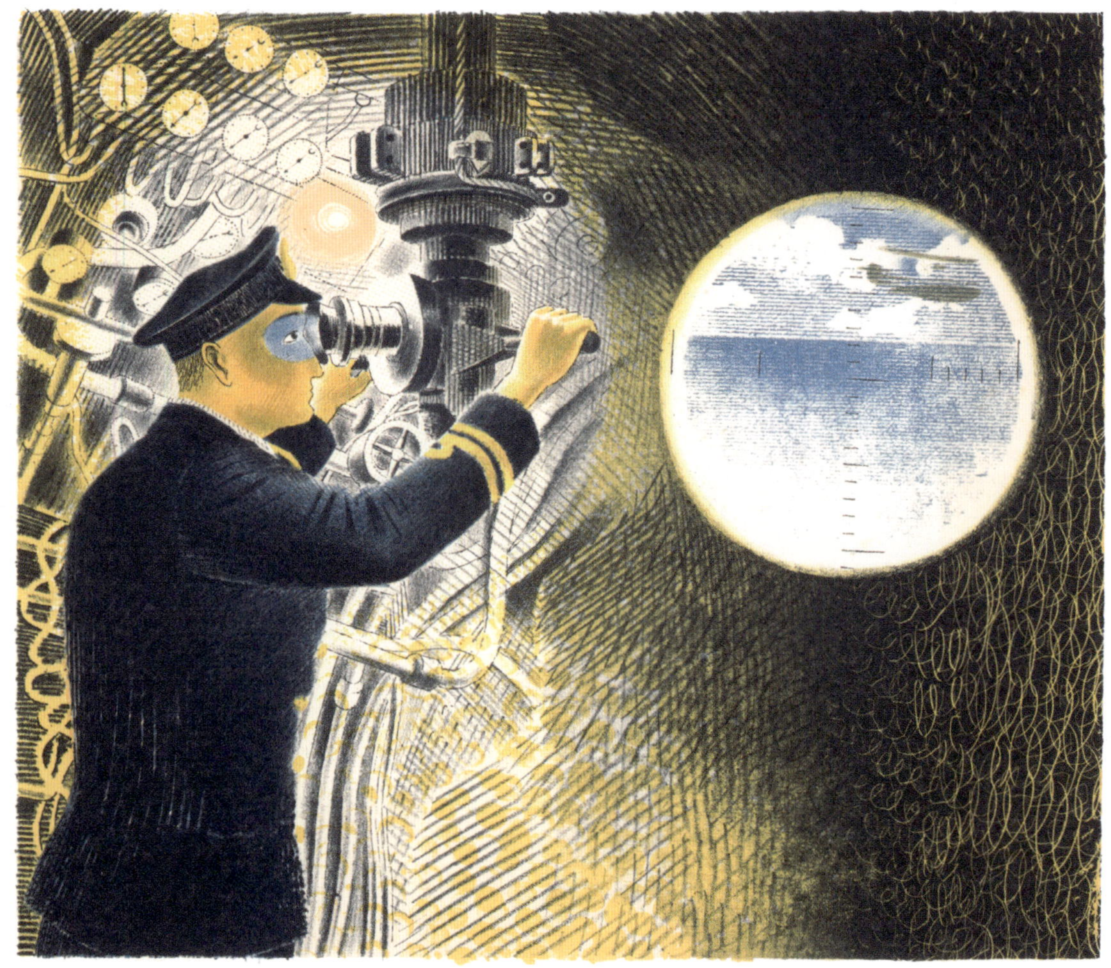

Commander at the Periscope

1940/1941

RAVILIOUS AND SUBMARINE DREAM

Peyton Skipwith, in his introduction to the book *Submarine Dream (Lithographs and Letters of Eric Ravilious,* edited by Brian Webb, published by the Camberwell Press) writes of Eric Ravilious as being one of the inter-war painters who were caught between extremes – 'the tyranny of abstraction on one hand and academic pedantry on the other' – and that really all Ravilious wanted to do was get on with his work, outside internecine art politics. Ravilious is variously appreciated as either an artist marginal to the mainstream of British 20th century art, or, on Francis Spalding's rating, the greatest water colourist, a worthy descendant of the greats – Girtin, Crome and Cotman.

Wherever he is placed, the story of his submarine lithographs, completed in the early part of World War Two, not long before his premature death ('presumed dead' when the plane that he was in failed to return from a flight over Iceland), is a tale of a still-young artist, perhaps satiated with his outpouring of wood engravings, and unsure of where to go next in his work; a tale of a war artist, held in limbo, neither free to experiment as he would have liked, nor fully employed on war-associated projects.

The pressure to make a contribution, in some way, to the war effort was immense, and many artists found themselves caught up in the intricacies of camouflage, the simplistic assumption being that 'visual' people could solve 'visual' problems. Perhaps with a similar naïve linkage, after considering the Artists' Rifles, Ravilious impulsively joined his local Observer Corps, based at Castle Hedingham in Essex.

More appropriately, in December 1939, he was appointed a war artist by the War Artists' Advisory Committee (WAAC). He was courted by the Admiralty to work for them in a letter from R. Gleadowe, formerly Slade Professor at Oxford, and now representing the navy on WAAC. Ravilious was appointed for six months in the Nore Command with the rank of Honorary Captain R.N. WAAC employed some thirty full-time artists at any one time and gave commissions to a further hundred, purchasing work already done from some two hundred others.

For a time Ravilious moved, or rather was moved, somewhat aimlessly, from Chatham to Sheerness to Grimsby, drawing escort vessels, destroyers and the like, but by July 1940 he found himself based at HMS Dolphin, the Gosport submarine base. It was from this posting that he was to be at his most impressively productive, making trips out of Gosport in submarines, accumulating numerous sketches, drawings and watercolours. It was much earlier in the year that he conceived the idea of producing – 'a set of six prints in a folio as pictures, not necessarily with any text; or simply picture prints and leave it at that.'

This project was thought of even before he had received his pass to move freely round the Gosport docks. He put the idea to WAAC but they had a totally different suggestion – the curious possibility of making a children's painting book from his submarine drawings!

Ravilious discussed the idea with Noel Carrington, with whom he had produced the now iconic book, *High Street*, just prior to the onset of war. The submarine drawings went to and fro across London from publisher to publisher, with no particularly enthusiastic response from any of them. Any such would have immediately been dampened down after Carrington had got a costing for a painting book from Geoffrey Smith. Carrington reported (December 1940):

> 'Geoffrey Smith's costing of the Painting Book 'Marine Interiors' for the size you want 11" by 12 ½" with a cover comes out at 11d even if you do 25,000, even at present paper prices. That would mean publishing at least at 2/6d which would put it out of the price so far as Lane was concerned...having to have colour opposite outline drawings on each page means printing both sides of the sheet in colour, which is unlike the Puffin books where every other spread is in black and white and only one side of the sheet is printed in colour.'

On receipt of this news Ravilious summarised the situation for WAAC:

> '...neither Curwen, Ripley, Murray or Lane can produce these pictures for all sorts of reasons, so I've abandoned the idea of a book and yesterday went to see the lithographic printers at Ipswich. They will produce the things simply as pictures in a small edition for 100 pounds; and if I can manage it this will be done...The Leicester Gallery say that they are willing to sell the lithographs if I produce them, so that with luck (if they are not bombed meanwhile), it may pay the expenses.'

Ravilious had got his way. Although he seems to have gone along with the idea of a children's painting book, he wrote his real feelings to his fellow artist Helen Binyon (December 1940):

> '...how fine not to have bloody publishers and no children's book either. Ipswich will print the things and I start work tomorrow.'

In letters to Carrington, Binyon and WAAC during the spring of 1941, Ravilious described the excitement and the frustrations of working on the lithographs – of experimenting along with Cowell's operatives as to what paper and lithographic tints to use; and of the fun he found from 'rolling bits on here and there which you do with a brass roller'; and the patience he needed waiting for the censor to clear the images as 'not likely to divulge secrets to the enemy'. His enjoyment was such that he recommends to Binyon the possibility of her working at Cowells, stressing his particular delight in his relationship with Smith:

> '...because he will take the trouble, and is nice and a socialist, also, so far, his works have not been hit by a bomb... I do enjoy working in this medium again.'

It seems that after his experiments at Ipswich, Ravilious prepared his lithographic plates at home, taking them to Ipswich for printing. As early as February 1941 Carrington wrote to Ravilious that Smith had shown him a few of the lithographs which Carrington rated as 'rich and fine', with the only proviso that they might have benefited from margins. Ravilious was not entirely happy with his work and confessed that he had, possibly, once or twice, been too rash in his experimenting. Eventually ten lithographs were printed showing submariners working a variety of machines and relaxing in their wardroom.

It is not recorded how many sets were printed, but certainly less than fifty. Sets very occasionally appear on the market, attracting five figure prices. Skipworth, one of the most notable commentators on the period, considered that Ravilious's drawings and watercolours, and the lithographs made from them as 'one of the most haunting and enduring series of images of World War Two'.

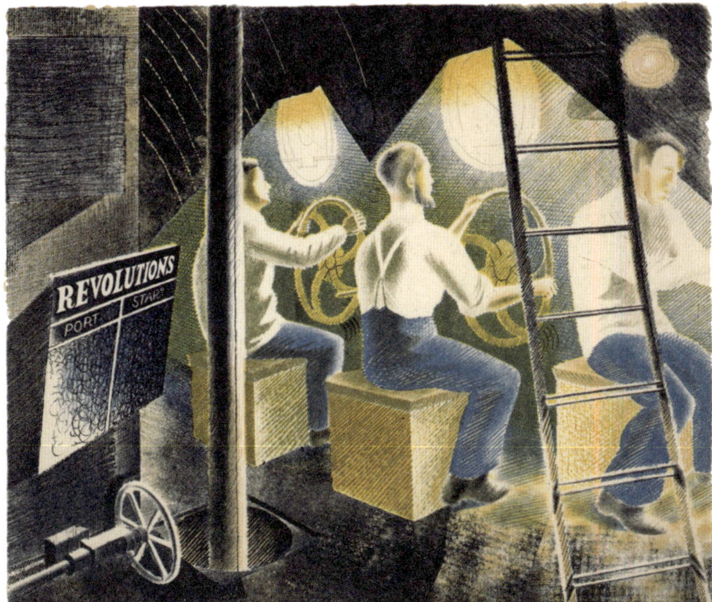

Diving Controls 1

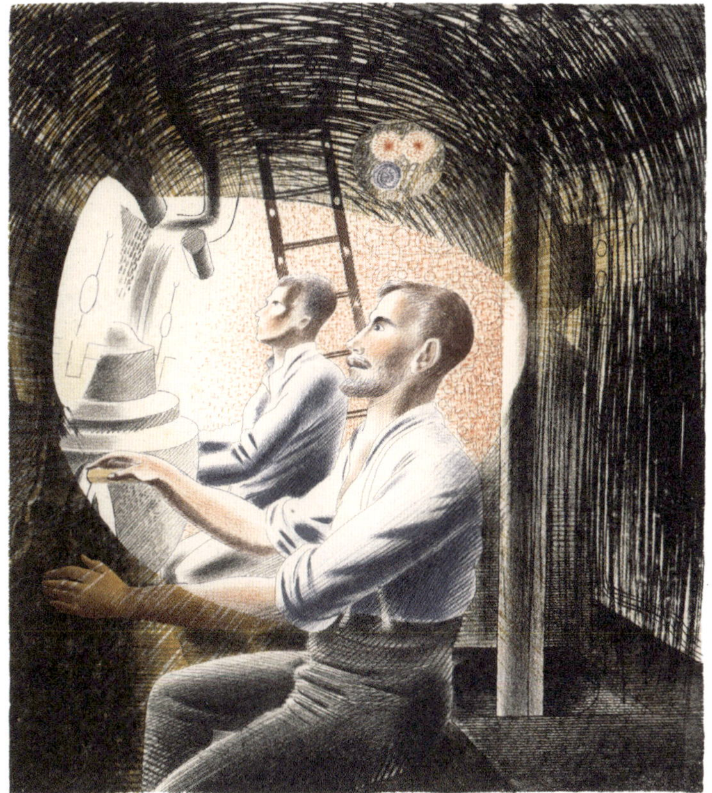

Diving Controls 2

1948

JOHN LEWIS AND A HANDBOOK OF PRINTING TYPES

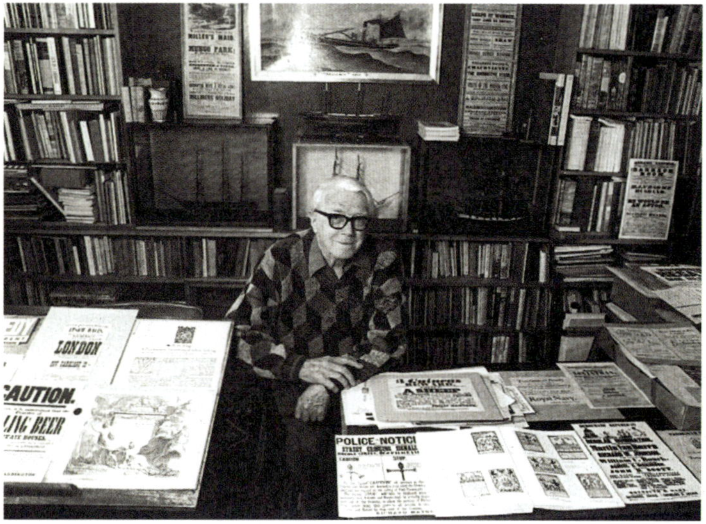

John Lewis and printed ephemera, photograph by Dominic Turner

John Lewis had trained as an illustrator at Goldsmiths College in the 1930s, and had begun to build up an independent practice, when his career was put on hold by the Second World War. As with so many other artists, the authorities, in their wisdom, thought camouflage the most suitable outlet for his talents.

When the war was coming to an end, Lewis began to consider how to develop his career, and it was his fellow camouflagers – Lynton Lamb and James Gardner, who helped him decide. Lamb suggested that book design would provide wider openings than illustration; and Gardner came up with a specific opening. Lewis remembered Gardner shouting across a room to him:

> 'I've just had an offer from the printers who did my Puffin books. They're up in East Anglia. They want to start a design studio. The job's no good to me – but I thought it might suit you.'

The estimation of suitability seems largely to have related to Lewis's love of sailing and to the fact that Cowells was in Ipswich, sailing country. When Lewis questioned Gardner further about the firm he got this description:

> 'It's an old-fashioned outfit. They run a shop and a wine business as well. They're basically lithographers and bloody

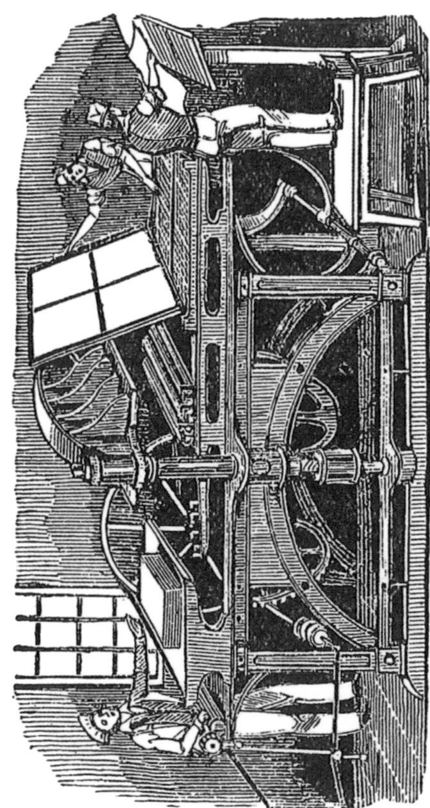

W. S. COWELL LIMITED

announce that

the publication date of

A

HANDBOOK

OF

PRINTING

TYPES

will be about

MAY 23rd, 1947

The Handbook will be obtainable
from the distributors
Messrs Faber and Faber Ltd London

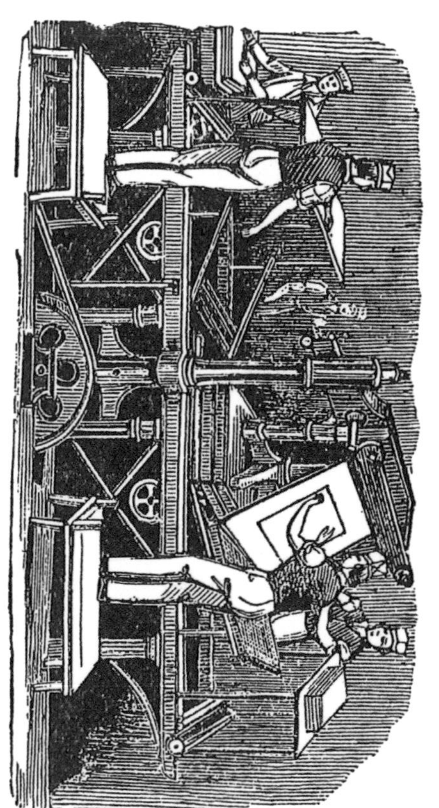

A Handbook of Printing Types *Advertisement, April 1947*

good colour printers. Geoffrey Smith, one of the bosses, is keen on turning them into book printers – I reckon that is something you could do for them.'

Lewis was interviewed, in London, by Eric Hanson, and, indeed, much of the interview consisted of a discussion of the navigational hazards of the river Deben. It was Hanson who suggested Lewis meeting up with Carrington, because of his experience with Cowells working on the Puffin Picture Books. Carrington reassured Lewis that his near total ignorance of book design would not be a handicap but could even be viewed as an advantage in bringing a fresh eye to the subject.

Lewis, the fresh-eyed amateur, then travelled to Ipswich to meet Smith who took him to see the litho-studios where, at that instance, the young Mervyn Peake was working on illustrations for *Bleak House* (not eventually published). Lewis was appointed to set up a design studio, but on the condition that he agreed to attend a short course at the London College of Printing.

Lewis joined Cowells in January 1946 and, what in recollection could well have been an exaggeration, was asked by Smith, immediately, to prepare a type-book illustrating what Cowells had on offer. Smith is reported to have added:

> '...something to show we are in the book market – the illustrated book market. A chap who was coming to us has done a little work on it. Here are his proofs. This will give you something to get your teeth into.'

Lewis's knowledge of type was minimal and he was to experience the steepest of learning curves – familiarising himself with Cowell's composing room, getting an historical perspective on the subject in Cowell's library, and visiting an ex-camouflage friend, Gabriel White, who was by then at the Arts Council. It was with White that Lewis discussed the possibility of having illustrations in his typebook (something of an innovation) and White was able to suggest names of possible artists to approach for this. Smith, at first, had been rather aghast at the idea, particularly as Lewis was keen to include artists that Smith considered rather 'modern'. However, when Lewis assured him that his 'moderns' were really distinguished, and that their inclusion would bring Cowells kudos, Smith accepted the idea. Smith had previously turned down one of Lewis's 'distinguished' when he had been offered Moore's *Shelter Sketchbook* which he had considered 'not really nice'.

Along with Moore, Lewis commissioned Graham Sutherland, John Piper, John Nash, Blair Hughes-Stanton and, on Carrington's suggestion, Barnett Freedman; they were all enthusiastic about contributing. Edward Bawden, however, when asked, refused to do an illustration for a suggested passage from *The Water Babies*, but decided merely to use some images of snails from a book he was working on at the time. Freedman, when asked, was amazed that Lewis was not aware of Oliver Simon's classy printing journal *Signature* and immediately, and with a good deal of Toad-like spluttering, rectified such ignorance by getting Lewis a copy. Stanley Morison, the typographer, greeted Lewis's naivety with a greater sensitivity and understanding than the bluff Freedman and exhorted him to 'Go Ahead!':

> 'I expect the book will be full of mistakes and it will cost your firm a lot of money, but there is just a chance that by doing something like this, you will learn your job.'

Illustration used as front cover for A Handbook of Printing Types

As Morison predicted, the book proved both full of mistakes and expensive, but it caused a considerable stir in the printing world by its novelty. Smith sent out copies of the book in all directions, and a file of some hundred and forty replies is now lodged in Lewis's archives at Reading University. A glance down the list of those who had bothered to reply provides a sample of the great and the good of the time – Sir Francis Meynell, Beatrice Warde, John Rothenstein, Stanley Unwin, Richard de la Mare, Allen Lane, Ashley Havinden, John Betjeman, Harold Curwen…

Many of the letters were merely acknowledgment of receipt, frequently with accompanying adjectives of oft extravagant praise – inspired, magnificent, imaginative, stimulating, without blemish, and so on. The fullest critiques came from Sean Jennet (later to write *The Making of Books*), John Heywood (the first editor of *The Book Collector*), and Stanley Hayter (whose letter heading stated baldly 'from Hayter, the typographer').

Some of the nit-picking related to the use of hyphens, apostrophes and the like. The aesthetics of the book were panned, by some as too modern, by others as too old-fashioned, as is usual when it comes to matters of taste. There were those who thought Lewis should have used young unknown artists rather than established ones. The cover was not universally liked (an old map of Suffolk with a composing stick super-imposed, the shadow of which pointed to Ipswich.) The reversal of the stick was thought to be muddling.

A more major criticism was the limited number of types actually included. Smith had told Lewis that he didn't want the expense of adding to his current list of Monotype faces, but that Lewis should just make the best of what they stocked. Lewis may have gained some comfort from the support he was given by Brooke Crutchley, then printer to the Cambridge University Press, who in his reply asserted:

> 'I approve very much of your attitude that nine well-selected composing founts are adequate for all normal purposes. We hold an appalling number of book founts and are setting about some rationalisation. I myself manage with seven: Modern (Monotype 7 series) Imprint, Plantin, Baskerville, Bembo, Times and Bell.'

Smith seems to have greeted praise and criticism with stoicism and, with his usual charm and diplomacy, told Lewis that he thought people had been most kind to have taken so much trouble over the book, and that any necessary corrections could be made in the next edition. The popularity of the book was such that a second enlarged (and corrected) edition was published in 1948.

For John Lewis, doing the book proved significant; he recorded that 'with that slightly imperfect little book as a starting point the pattern of my future was fashioned.'

Lewis went from Cowells to the Royal College of Art where his practical exercises with the students on book production grew into the Lion & Unicorn Press; and from there he went to Studio Vista, where he worked on over forty books. He, himself, wrote and designed a similar number, not only on typography and book design, but on sailing, and, with his wife Griselda, on Pratt Ware ceramics, of which they were major collectors.

For some years Lewis continued his connection with Cowells on a consultative basis and many of his own books, certainly those concerned with book design, were printed there, and for some of these Cowells acted as publisher as well as printer. On the back of Smith's ambitions for Cowells, Lewis was enabled to build up a career that made him one of the best known people in book design and typography of his generation.

Although Cowells made various further stabs at working with an internal art director after Lewis had left, they eventually appear to have left the role to those of their printers who showed any artistic bent, as, for example with Maurice Walker who became a typographical specialist and Peter Ling; a good example of his work was Cowell's printing of the Sotheby Park Bernet Publications book celebrating the centenary of Sir Alfred Munnings.

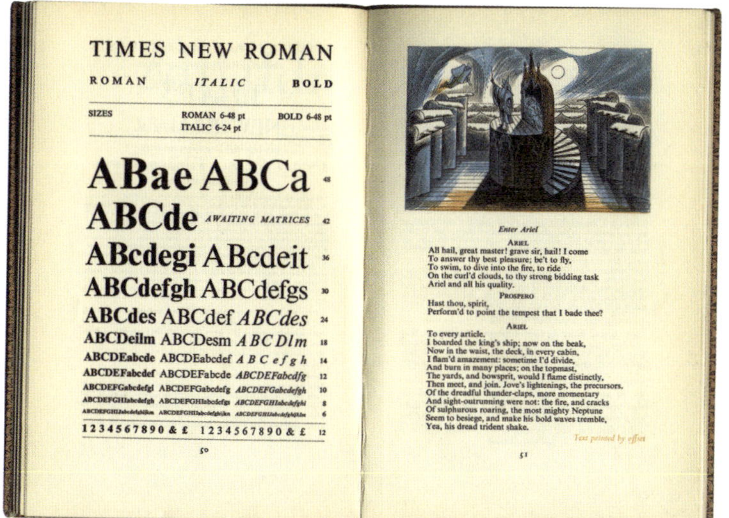

TIMES NEW ROMAN

ROMAN *ITALIC* BOLD

SIZES ROMAN 6-48 pt ITALIC 6-24 pt BOLD 6-48 pt

ABae ABCa 48
ABCde *AWAITING MATRICES* 42
ABcdegi ABcdeit 36
ABCdefgh ABCdefgs 30
ABCdes ABCdef *ABCdes* 24
ABCDeilm ABCDesm *A B C Dlm* 18
ABCDEabcde ABCDEabcdef *A B C e f g h* 14
ABCDEFabcdef ABCDEFabcde *ABCDEFabcdfg* 12
ABCDEFGabcdefgi ABCDEFGabcdefg *ABCDEFGabcdefgh* 10
ABCDEFGHIabcdefgh ABCDEFGHIabcdefgs *ABCDEFGHIabcdefghi* 8
[illegible] 6
1 2 3 4 5 6 7 8 9 0 & £ 1 2 3 4 5 6 7 8 9 0 & £ 12

50

Enter Ariel

ARIEL
All hail, great master! grave sir, hail! I come
To answer thy best pleasure; be't to fly,
To swim, to dive into the fire, to ride
On the curl'd clouds, to thy strong bidding task
Ariel and all his quality.

PROSPERO
Hast thou, spirit,
Perform'd to point the tempest that I bade thee?

ARIEL
To every article.
I boarded the king's ship; now on the beak,
Now in the waist, the deck, in every cabin,
I flam'd amazement: sometime I'd divide,
And burn in many places; on the topmast,
The yards, and bowsprit, would I flame distinctly,
Then meet, and join. Jove's lightenings, the precursors,
Of the dreadful thunder-claps, more momentary
And sight-outrunning were not: the fire, and cracks
Of sulphurous roaring, the most mighty Neptune
Seem to besiege, and make his bold waves tremble,
Yea, his dread trident shake.

Text printed by offset

51

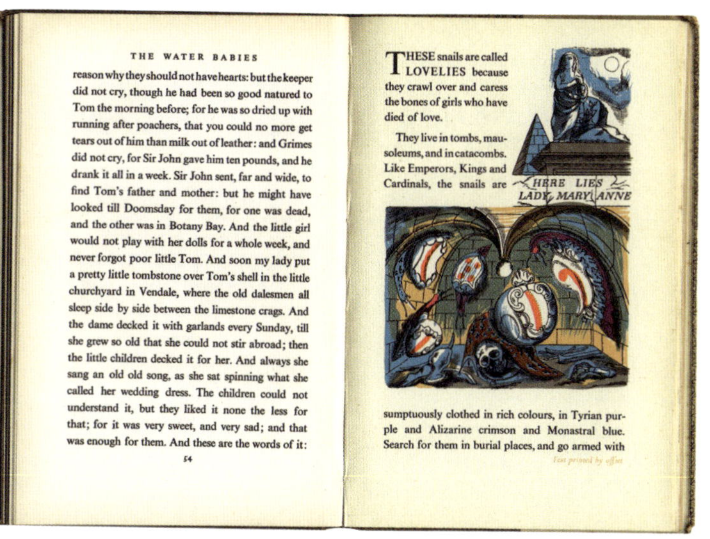

THE WATER BABIES

reason why they should not have hearts: but the keeper did not cry, though he had been so good natured to Tom the morning before; for he was so dried up with running after poachers, that you could no more get tears out of him than milk out of leather: and Grimes did not cry, for Sir John gave him ten pounds, and he drank it all in a week. Sir John sent, far and wide, to find Tom's father and mother: but he might have looked till Doomsday for them, for one was dead, and the other was in Botany Bay. And the little girl would not play with her dolls for a whole week, and never forgot poor little Tom. And soon my lady put a pretty little tombstone over Tom's shell in the little churchyard in Vendale, where the old dalesmen all sleep side by side between the limestone crags. And the dame decked it with garlands every Sunday, till she grew so old that she could not stir abroad; then the little children decked it for her. And always she sang an old old song, as she sat spinning what she called her wedding dress. The children could not understand it, but they liked it none the less for that; for it was very sweet, and very sad; and that was enough for them. And these are the words of it:

54

THESE snails are called LOVELIES because they crawl over and caress the bones of girls who have died of love.

They live in tombs, mausoleums, and in catacombs. Like Emperors, Kings and Cardinals, the snails are

sumptuously clothed in rich colours, in Tyrian purple and Alizarine crimson and Monastral blue. Search for them in burial places, and go armed with

Specimen pages from A Handbook of Printing Types, *1947,*
with illustrations by Edward Bawden (right)

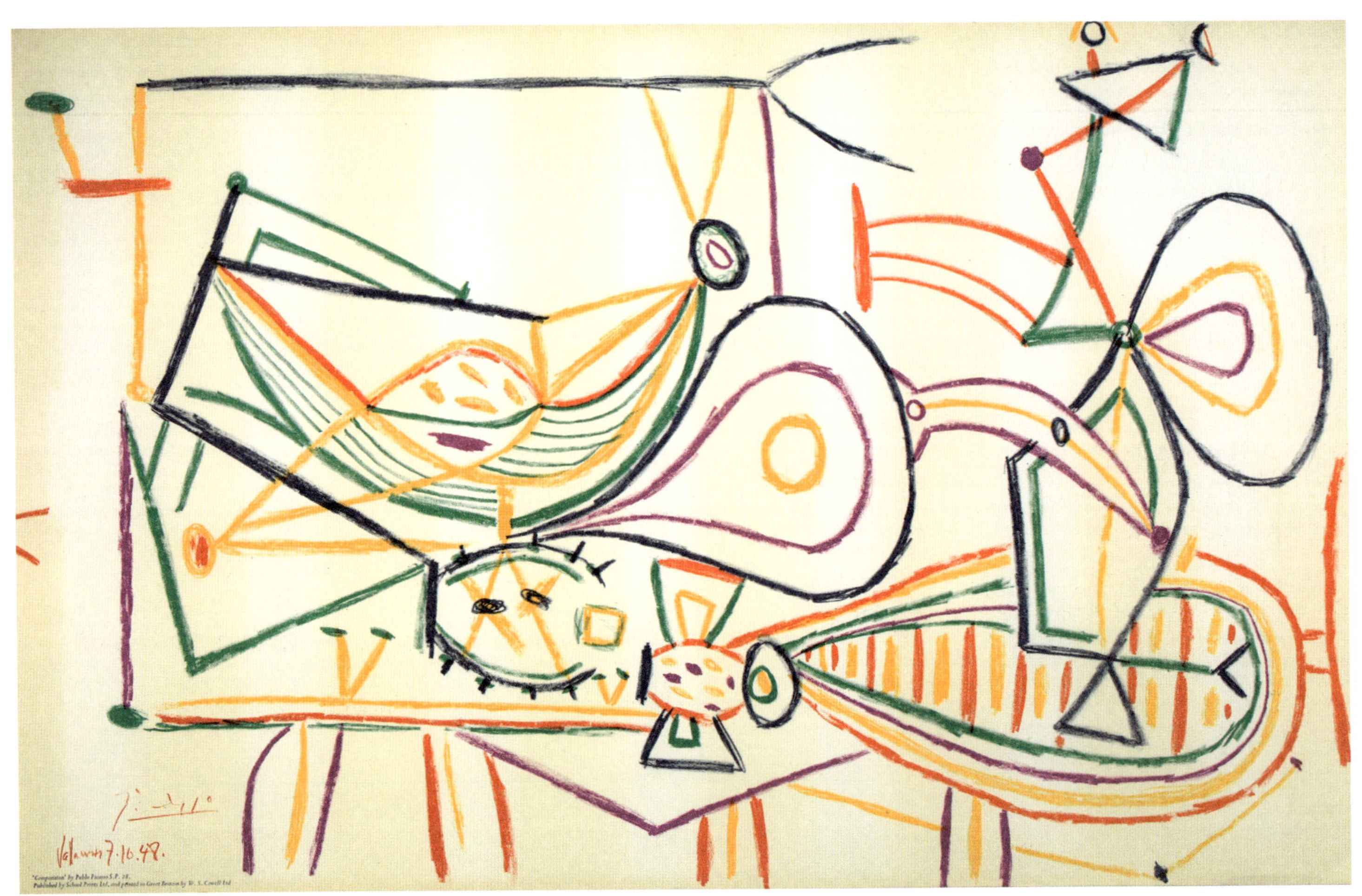

Composition *by Picasso*

1948

THE SCHOOL PRINTS

In 1948 Geoffrey Smith was contacted by a young war widow, Brenda Rawnsley, who wanted to explore the possibility of Cowells helping her with an ambitious project on which she was determined.

Her husband, filled with the idealism of a middle class youth, had, just prior to the war, begun to develop a scheme for introducing children to 'good' art by having relatively cheap reproduced works of the 'masters' distributed to schools. He and his young war bride, when they had fleetingly got together between their various wartime escapades across North and East Africa and the Middle East, talked about how his missionary ideas could be developed after the war.

The widow, left to build a life for herself, decided to resurrect her late husband's project, and, with very little knowledge of art, or of how the art world functioned, but with lots of energy, charm and sheer chutzpah, had, within two years of the war ending, commissioned some twenty-four artists, mainly British, to provide lithographed prints. These were not only sold to educational establishments and places of work, but could be bought for home decoration!

Brenda, a debutante brought up at the Egyptian court, began to be bored with such a parochial essay and set her sights on more international artists who might provide works 'pour les enfants du monde'. With Picasso, Leger, Matisse, Dufy and Braque in mind, this was no easy ambition, particularly in post-war conditions of material rationing and restricted foreign exchange, let alone an unknown approaching these art world 'gods'. And then there was the technical problem, even if she could persuade such artists to her cause, of how to get auto-lithographed plates transported across the Channel. Certainly this was not possible with stones or zinc plates. It was at this point that she contacted Cowells.

Brenda could not recollect how Cowells had come into the picture but thought it was through her loaning prints to ICI Plastics. For her earlier *School Prints* Brenda had worked with Thomas Griffits at the Baynard Press, but Smith was able to persuade her to move to Cowells on the strength of Plastocowell which could solve her 'transport' problems with her European artists. Smith visited Brenda at her little gallery in Motcomb Street to show her the *Orlando* books as examples of what could be achieved with Plastocowell. These impressed her tremendously by their colourfulness and she decided to give the material a trial run. For this purpose, with no false modesty, she settled on Henry Moore, who she possibly knew through his friend, Herbert Read, an advisor to the *School Prints.*

Brenda wrote to Moore with a girlish feverish enthusiasm (15th July 1948):

> 'Would you have time to go over to Ipswich? Do you know about the plastic process? Would you like us to send you the plates? Would you like me to bring the plates down? What would you like?'

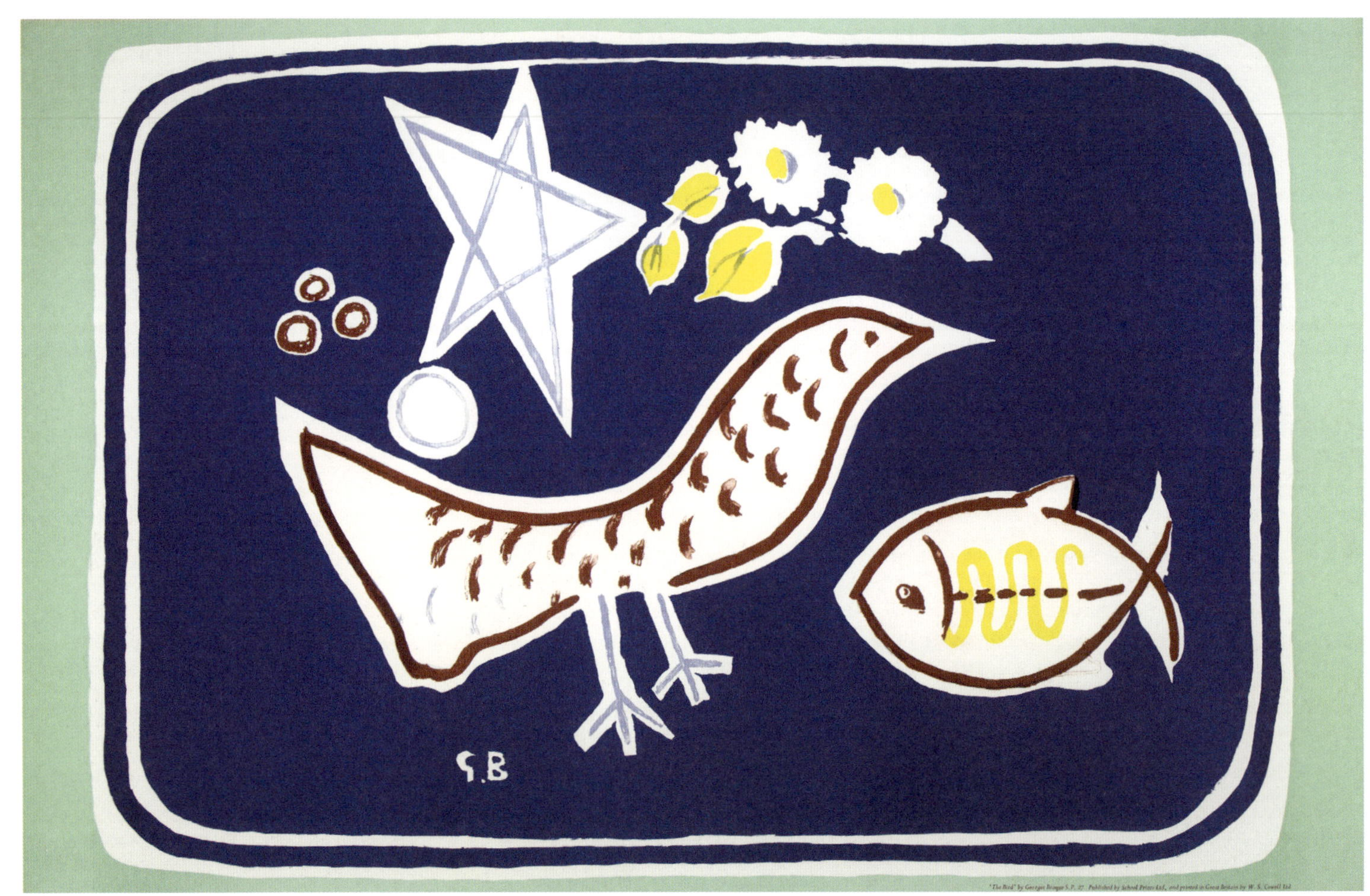

The Bird *by Braque*

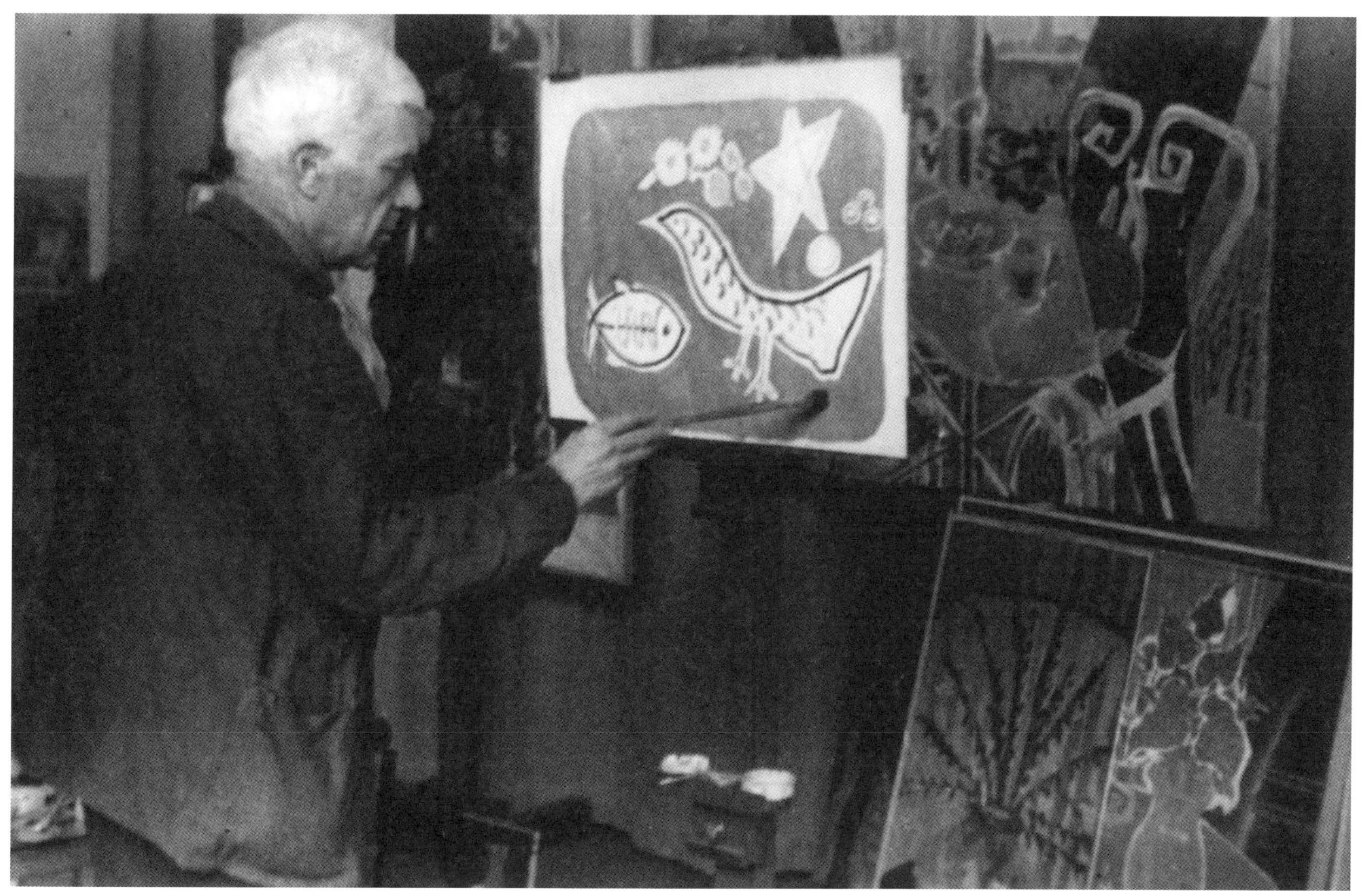

Georges Braque painting The Bird

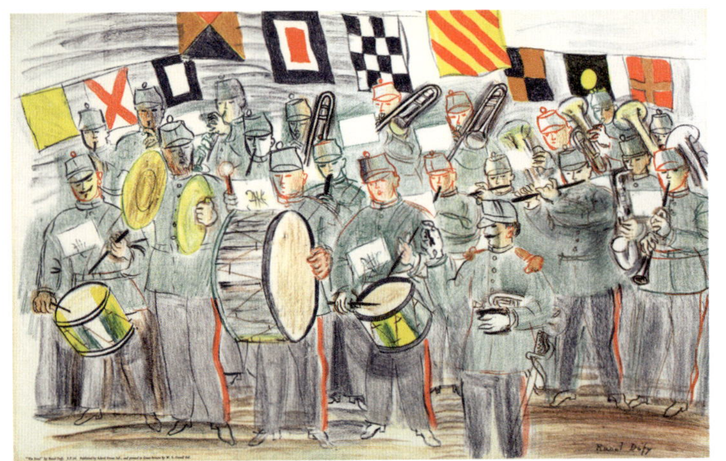

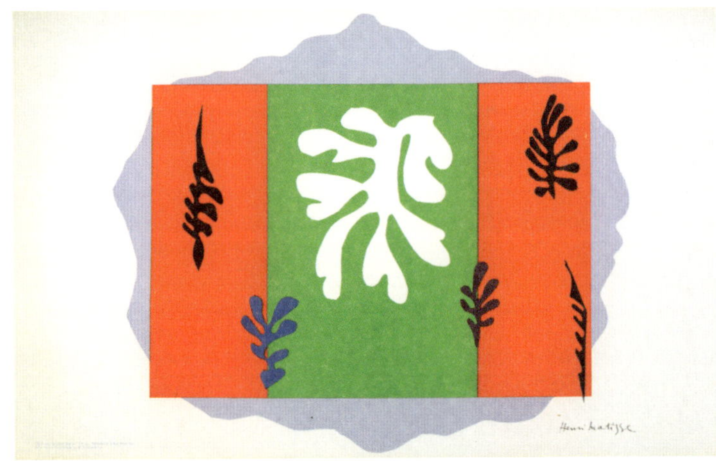

The Band *by Raoul Dufy (left),* The Dancer *by Henri Matisse (right)*
and King of Hearts *by Fernand Léger (opposite page)*

Brenda said that she eventually got Moore to go down with her to Cowells, with his sketch book, to put two drawings on to Plastocowell; he gave it his approval. Brenda, however, had one nagging doubt, which she kept to herself:

> '...clearly Cowells felt, and I think knew all along that they (the Plastocowell sheets) would have to be photographed through onto zinc plates for printing. This raised doubts, in the end, as to whether my lithographs were really original, but I claim they are, for the artists drew each colour on a separate plate.'

With Moore agreeing to do a large lithograph, Brenda set out to persuade her other 'masters' to provide works for her scheme. Geoffrey Smith found himself swept up into a small group accompanying her, in a tiny plane, to Paris. In her old age Brenda would claim that this was Smith's first trip abroad; this seems surprising, but if it were so, then the whole spree must have seemed like a mad escapade to the Ipswich printer.

Smith was presumably included because of Brenda's limited technical know-how, and in order to sell the idea of Plastocowell to the artists. He also seems to have had other uses, for when they ran out of money in Marseille he had a contact with a local banker. Their amazing trip, which included visits to Braque, Leger and Matisse in Paris, and Picasso and Dufy in the South of France has been well documented. What Smith thought of the whole affair is not documented!

In the eventuality Picasso, Dufy, Leger and Braque all worked on the plates, but Matisse, ill and frail, fell back on making

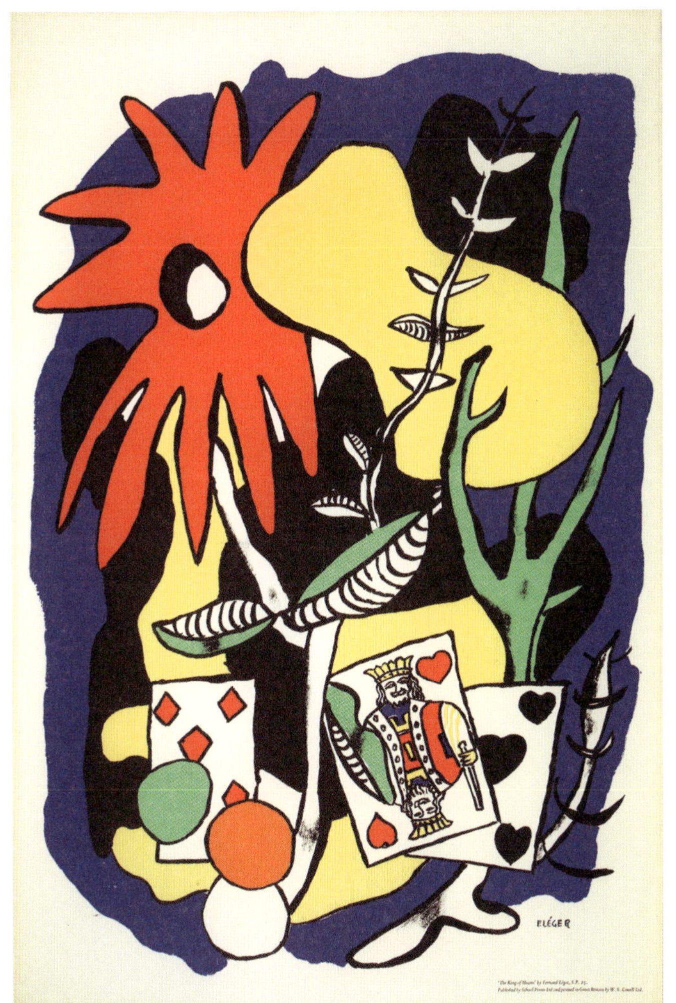

paper cut-outs. Besides such problems as obtaining import duties for the plates, finding cartridge cases for their transport, and rushing from the airport to Ipswich herself to ensure they arrived on time, some technical hitches occurred. Dufy, for one, was not entirely happy with the paper being used to print his lithograph:

> 'Si vous pouviez tirer sur du papier plus blanc que celui que vous m'avez montre les images y gagneraient.'

And Matisse worried that Cowells would not achieve the exact colours he had chosen:

> '...if the depth of colour of the red and green was correctly contrasted and you ran your eye down a straight line, the white dancers will actually dance; if there was any variation in the contrasting tones of the green and red, they would not dance.'

Leger and Cowells had some correspondence as to what was the correct order for printing his colours; and Dufy just did not seem able to get his pressure quite right, giving his print a rather faded look, but that was let pass.

For all these to-ings and fro-ings John Lewis seems to have been the point of contact for Brenda and her artists. Lewis was to write of the occasion, when he and his wife, Griselda, were going to the South of France on their first post-war holiday, that Smith persuaded him to combine business with pleasure by calling on Picasso who was behind with his offering:

> 'If you want an excuse, we have some long metal cylinders in which he can pack his rolled up drawings to send us.'

Lewis failed to return with the required package, but his encounter with Picasso (as with Brenda, taking place on the beach) must have had some effect, for the work arrived within the month.

For the launch of the 'European' *School Prints* all the six prints were exhibited along with examples of work on Plastocowell and Henry Moore's six progressives. Cowells also showed the prints as examples of their colour reproduction at the British Council's book exhibition in Helsinki in 1949.

That the prints were not the financial success that Brenda had hoped for, and that she got herself into endless arguments as to their 'original' status is recorded elsewhere. The commission had added considerably to Cowell's reputation, particularly as the plastic sheets, upon which the artists had drawn, were given by Brenda to the Tate Gallery for 'safe-keeping'; she, herself, kept Moore's original test pieces.

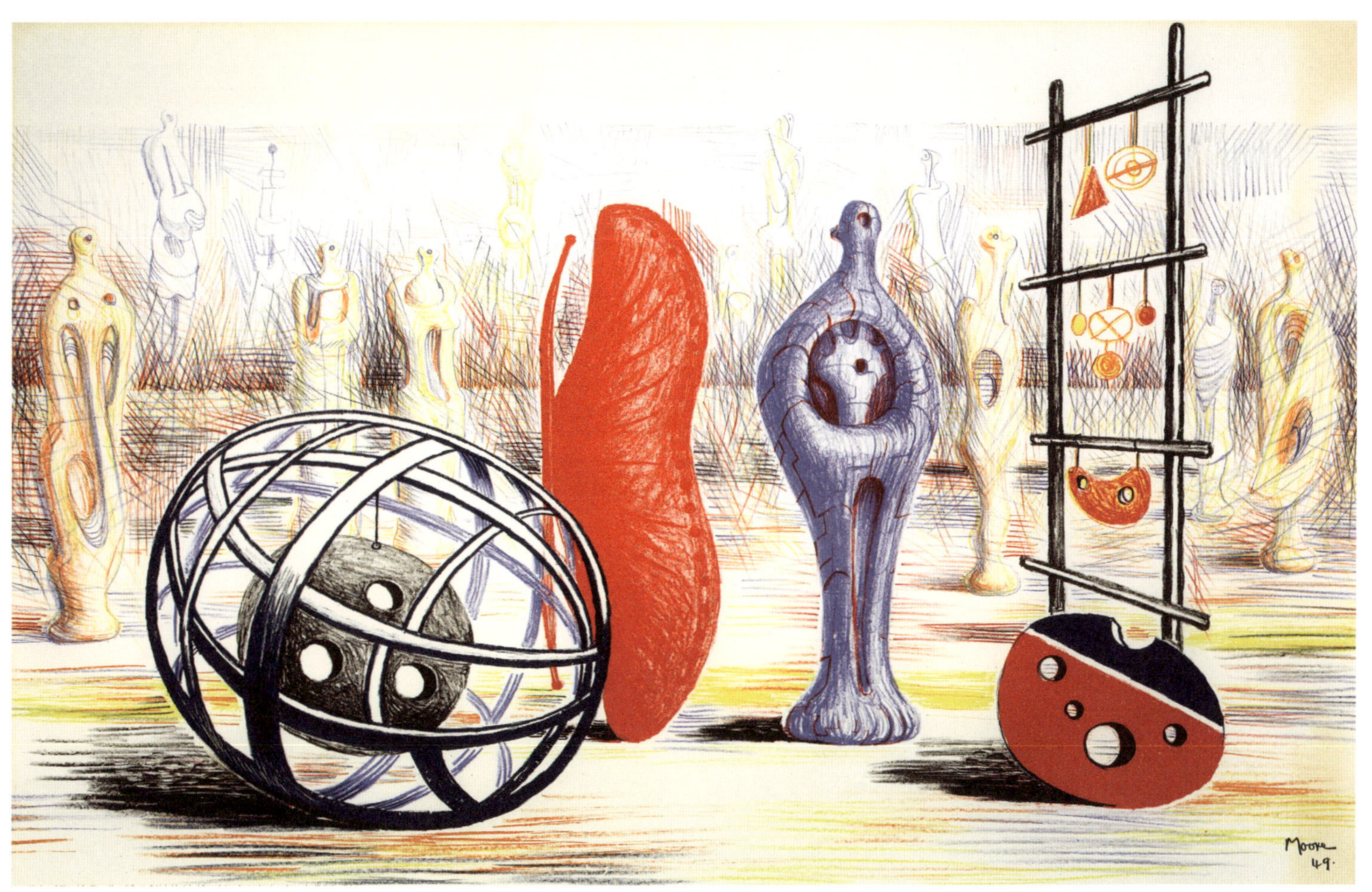

Sculptural Objects *by Henry Moore*

1948

THE ALDEBURGH FESTIVAL PROGRAMME

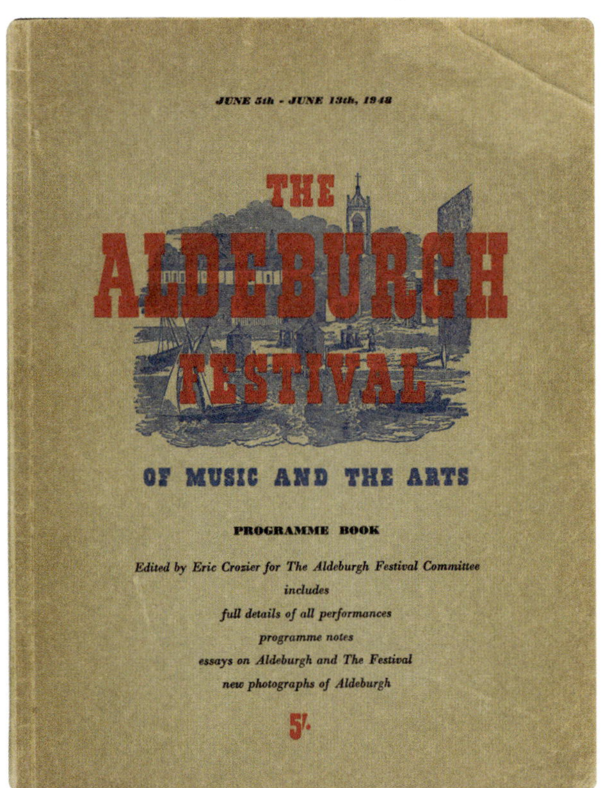

Programme for The Aldeburgh Festival, *June 1948*

Early in 1948, John Piper contacted John Lewis to ask whether Cowells could help a recently established committee that was planning a festival to be held in Aldeburgh, Suffolk. Smith, when consulted, was enthusiastic not only because it sounded a profitable commission but because he was very much an East Anglian, interested in everything going on in the region. The committee needed programmes, posters and other printed material and very shortly Benjamin Britten, with his entourage of Peter Pears, Eric Crozier and Elizabeth Sweeting (to become the first Festival manager) arrived at Cowells.

Subsequent meetings were held at Crag House, Aldeburgh and Lewis was not only drawn in to design the required ephemera and to act as Cowell's liaison man, but was persuaded to join the selection committee for the Festival's proposed art exhibition, alongside John Nash, John Piper and Philip James of the Arts Council. It was through this commission that Lewis was later to do the sets and costumes for Britten's *Let's Make an Opera.*

Lewis, enthusiastic about Victorian playbills and the like, consequently festooned the first Festival programme with wood-engravings and etchings of old Aldeburgh – coastline scenes and churches. This was to tie in nicely with the Committee's concern to make the Festival programme 'an Aldeburgh affair'. The Earl of Harewood, the Festival's first President, wrote, a shade grandiosely, in his introduction to the programme:

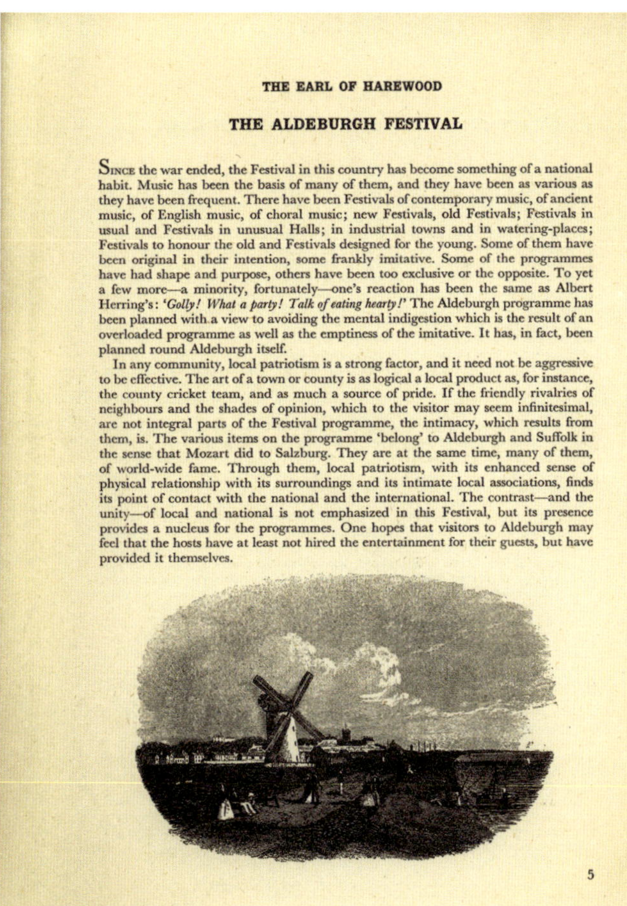

THE EARL OF HAREWOOD

THE ALDEBURGH FESTIVAL

SINCE the war ended, the Festival in this country has become something of a national habit. Music has been the basis of many of them, and they have been as various as they have been frequent. There have been Festivals of contemporary music, of ancient music, of English music, of choral music; new Festivals, old Festivals; Festivals in usual and Festivals in unusual Halls; in industrial towns and in watering-places; Festivals to honour the old and Festivals designed for the young. Some of them have been original in their intention, some frankly imitative. Some of the programmes have had shape and purpose, others have been too exclusive or the opposite. To yet a few more—a minority, fortunately—one's reaction has been the same as Albert Herring's: *'Golly! What a party! Talk of eating hearty!'* The Aldeburgh programme has been planned with a view to avoiding the mental indigestion which is the result of an overloaded programme as well as the emptiness of the imitative. It has, in fact, been planned round Aldeburgh itself.

In any community, local patriotism is a strong factor, and it need not be aggressive to be effective. The art of a town or county is as logical a local product as, for instance, the county cricket team, and as much a source of pride. If the friendly rivalries of neighbours and the shades of opinion, which to the visitor may seem infinitesimal, are not integral parts of the Festival programme, the intimacy, which results from them, is. The various items on the programme 'belong' to Aldeburgh and Suffolk in the sense that Mozart did to Salzburg. They are at the same time, many of them, of world-wide fame. Through them, local patriotism, with its enhanced sense of physical relationship with its surroundings and its intimate local associations, finds its point of contact with the national and the international. The contrast—and the unity—of local and national is not emphasized in this Festival, but its presence provides a nucleus for the programmes. One hopes that visitors to Aldeburgh may feel that the hosts have at least not hired the entertainment for their guests, but have provided it themselves.

5

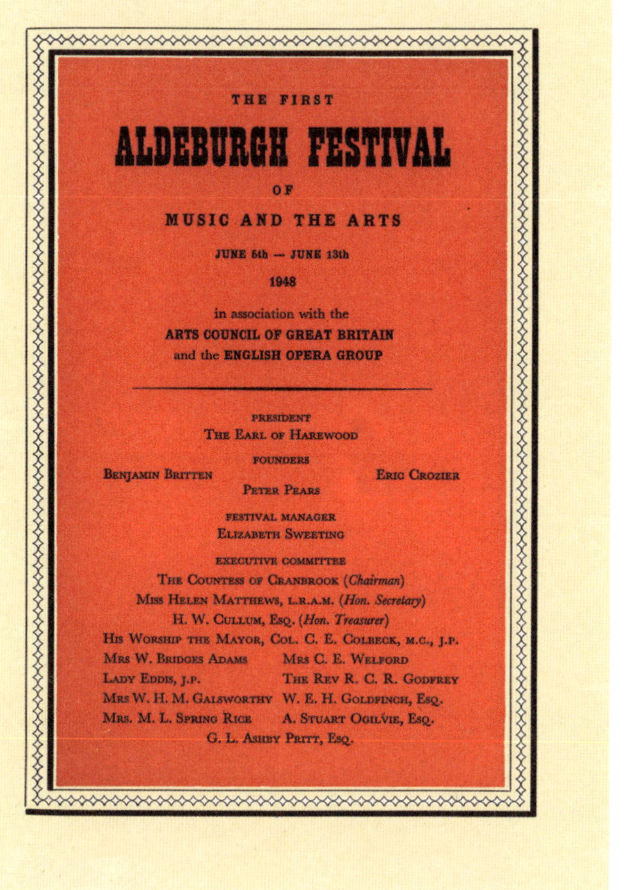

THE FIRST

ALDEBURGH FESTIVAL

OF

MUSIC AND THE ARTS

JUNE 6th — JUNE 13th

1948

in association with the

ARTS COUNCIL OF GREAT BRITAIN

and the ENGLISH OPERA GROUP

PRESIDENT

THE EARL OF HAREWOOD

FOUNDERS

BENJAMIN BRITTEN — PETER PEARS — ERIC CROZIER

FESTIVAL MANAGER

ELIZABETH SWEETING

EXECUTIVE COMMITTEE

THE COUNTESS OF CRANBROOK (*Chairman*)

MISS HELEN MATTHEWS, L.R.A.M. (*Hon. Secretary*)

H. W. CULLUM, ESQ. (*Hon. Treasurer*)

HIS WORSHIP THE MAYOR, COL. C. E. COLBECK, M.C., J.P.

MRS W. BRIDGES ADAMS — MRS C. E. WELFORD

LADY EDDIS, J.P. — THE REV R. C. R. GODFREY

MRS W. H. M. GALSWORTHY — W. E. H. GOLDFINCH, ESQ.

MRS. M. L. SPRING RICE — A. STUART OGILVIE, ESQ.

G. L. ASHBY PRITT, ESQ.

The Aldeburgh Festival Programme, *1948*

> 'In any community, the local patriotism is a strong factor… The various items on the programme 'belong' to Aldeburgh and Suffolk in the same sense that Mozart belonged to Salzburg.'

In contrast to Harewood's local patriotism and Lewis's nostalgia, included in the programme are eight photographs of Aldeburgh done by Bill Brandt, born in Germany and trained in Paris with Man Ray. Piper handed the photographs over to Lewis saying:

> 'I'm sure you'll produce something worth that (the suggested programme price of five shillings), particularly with these!'

The programme was edited by Eric Crozier who, when everything was printed and delivered on time, wrote to Lewis:

> 'Everyone loves the Programme Book and the other things you have done. You can be the Festival Typographic Designer in perpetuity.'

Smith, to sponsor the Festival, and as a useful public relations exercise for Cowells, laid on a large party at the Old Neptune, George Scott's mediaeval house, near Ipswich Docks. Numerous publishers were invited, along with every artist who had been printed at Cowells. In addition to the Ipswich reception guests were taken to a concert at Aldeburgh. The whole affair was such a success that it was repeated the following year.

In the circumstances Lewis did not become 'Typographic Designer in perpetuity'. He was to design the first seven programmes, and, later, number thirteen. He found Britten tricky to deal with, with ever changing favourites and outcasts, likes and dislikes. And Cowells were also dropped when Benhams, a Colchester printer, persuaded the Committee that they could reduce costs by cutting out the need for a designer and by them carrying out the printing at a cheaper rate. It may have been sour grapes, but Lewis thought Benham's efforts altogether inferior, particularly for the colour work.

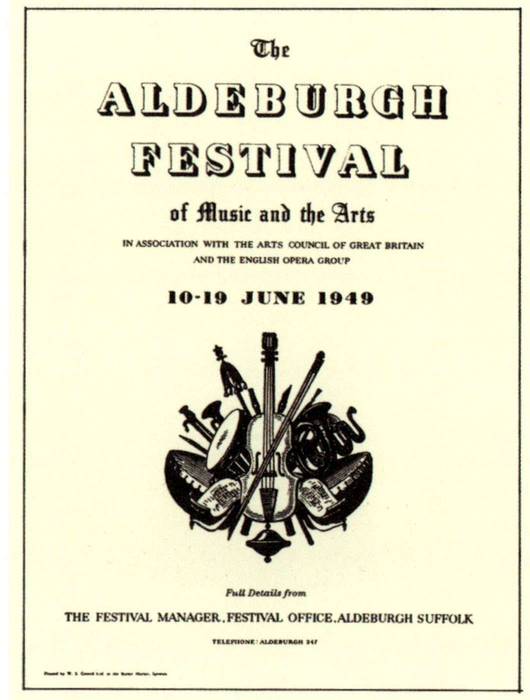

The second Aldeburgh Festival Poster, 1949

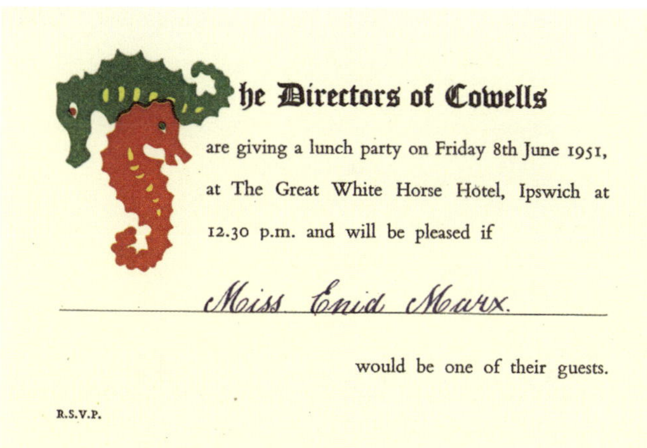

The Directors of Cowells are giving a lunch party on Friday 8th June 1951, at The Great White Horse Hotel, Ipswich at 12.30 p.m. and will be pleased if

Miss Enid Marx.

would be one of their guests.

R.S.V.P.

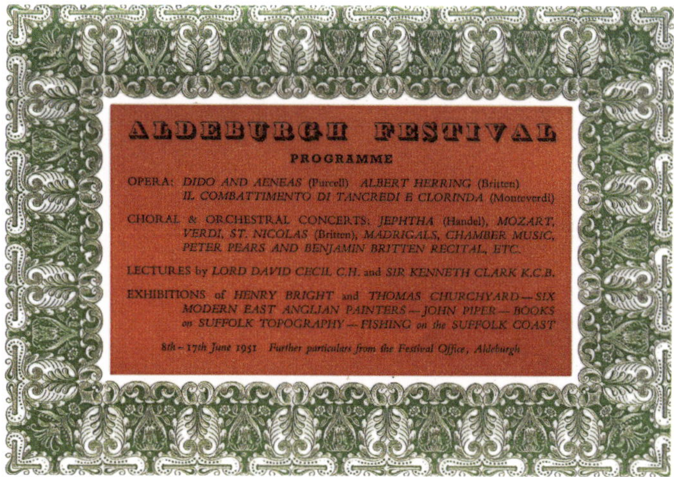

ALDEBURGH FESTIVAL

PROGRAMME

OPERA: *DIDO AND AENEAS* (Purcell) *ALBERT HERRING* (Britten) *IL COMBATTIMENTO DI TANCREDI E CLORINDA* (Monteverdi)

CHORAL & ORCHESTRAL CONCERTS: *JEPHTHA* (Handel), *MOZART, VERDI, ST. NICOLAS* (Britten), *MADRIGALS, CHAMBER MUSIC, PETER PEARS AND BENJAMIN BRITTEN RECITAL, ETC.*

LECTURES by *LORD DAVID CECIL C.H.* and *SIR KENNETH CLARK K.C.B.*

EXHIBITIONS of *HENRY BRIGHT* and *THOMAS CHURCHYARD—SIX MODERN EAST ANGLIAN PAINTERS—JOHN PIPER—BOOKS on SUFFOLK TOPOGRAPHY—FISHING on the SUFFOLK COAST*

8th–17th June 1951 Further particulars from the Festival Office, Aldeburgh

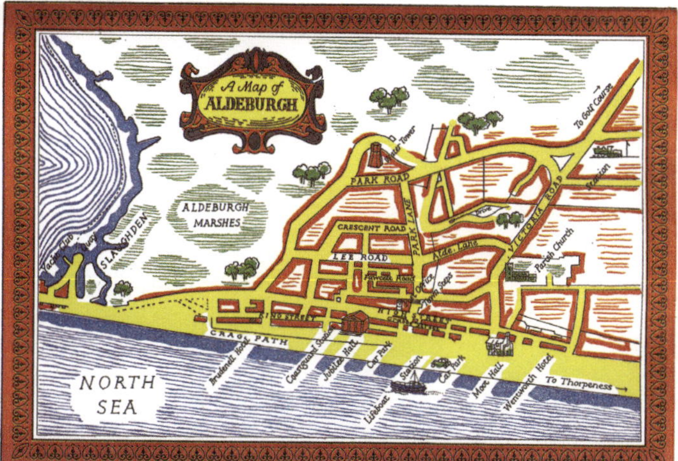

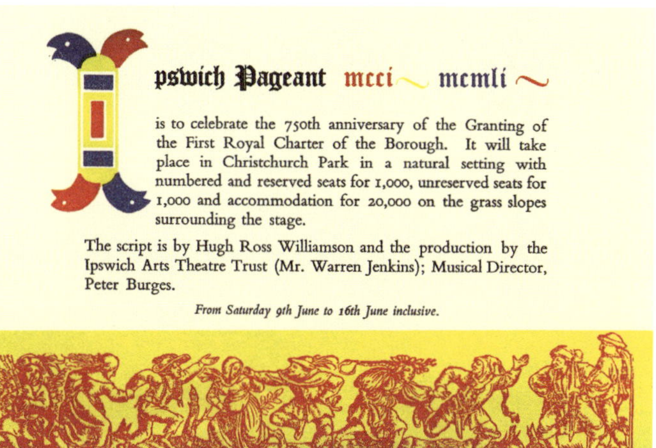

Ipswich Pageant mcci ~ mcmli ~

is to celebrate the 750th anniversary of the Granting of the First Royal Charter of the Borough. It will take place in Christchurch Park in a natural setting with numbered and reserved seats for 1,000, unreserved seats for 1,000 and accommodation for 20,000 on the grass slopes surrounding the stage.

The script is by Hugh Ross Williamson and the production by the Ipswich Arts Theatre Trust (Mr. Warren Jenkins); Musical Director, Peter Burges.

From Saturday 9th June to 16th June inclusive.

Enid Marx's invitation to the Aldeburgh Festival, 1951

THE ROYAL

PHILATELIC

COLLECTION

BY

SIR JOHN WILSON Bt

KEEPER OF THE ROYAL PHILATELIC COLLECTION

EDITOR

CLARENCE WINCHESTER

PUBLISHED BY

THE VISCOUNT KEMSLEY

at

THE DROPMORE PRESS LTD LONDON ENGLAND

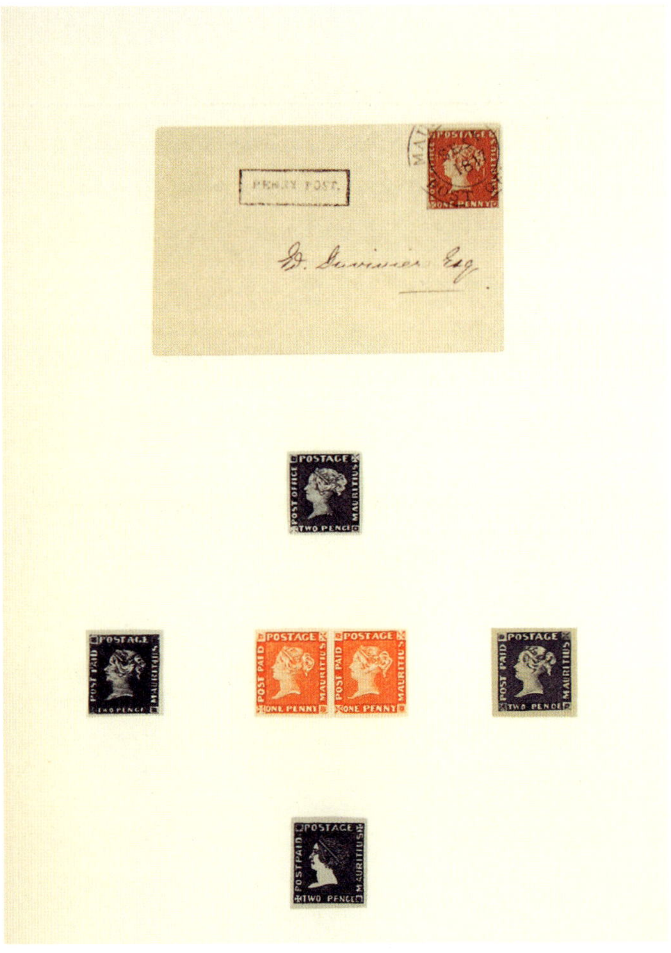

The Royal Philatelic Collection *by Sir John Wilson, 1952*

1952

THE ROYAL PHILATELIC COLLECTION

There can be few books, apart from those of the Fine Presses, where the printer of the book is referred to in the introductory pages. And even more rare is the book where the craftsmen at the printers are mentioned specifically by name. Such a book is *The Royal Philatelic Collection* which, when published, was variously described as the heaviest (fourteen and a half pounds), the most expensive (sixty guineas), with the highest number of overprints for some of its pages (fifty), and as guaranteed an unlimited life (at least 250 years). These superlatives were for a volume describing the history of, and current contents of, the stamp collection held at Buckingham Palace. The book was written by Sir John Wilson, Keeper of the King's Stamps, edited and designed by Clarence Winchester, published by Viscount Kemsely's Dropmore Press, and printed by W.S. Cowell Ltd.

The first adhesive stamp was issued in Great Britain on the 6th May 1840. At first stamp collecting was considered an activity for schoolboys and cranks, but by 1869 the London Philatelic Society had been founded (later to become the Royal Philatelic Society) and stamp collecting became serious. Collecting was now a matter for intense, nay academically-minded amateurs (who may, or may not, have been cranky), for dealers (who were quick to realise the financial returns on rarities, misprints, and the like), and still for schoolboys (and there may well have been the odd schoolgirl).

George V was such a schoolboy. An order form, dated 1864, exists, sent from the Palace to the firm Perkins, Bacon & Company (the government printers of the time) to provide specimens of the 1d black which had ceased to be current in 1841. These were to be 'reprints' for the amusement of the younger members of the Royal Family, and so started the Royal collection. The young George V, as Prince of Wales, inherited an on-going pursuit. At first he collected widely, but soon realised the impracticality of this and chose to concentrate on the British Empire and its Protectorates.

Of course he was in a favoured position, not only because of his purse, but because he was given precedence with all new issues from the Post Office and the Crown Agents for the Colonies. And dealers soon learnt to look to him when important stamp collections came on to the market. Then there were presents from friends, and even strangers, albeit, with the latter, stamps were offered in fair exchange as it was not protocol to receive such gifts. In his collecting George V was guided by his distinguished Keeper, Sir Edward Denny Bacon.

But George V was not merely a passive recipient but an active enthusiast. He would regularly set time aside for his stamps, in later life, three afternoons a week. He would visit the stamp printers, De La Rue, to keep abreast of technical developments in stamp production and would personally instruct the buying of stamps, having perused auction catalogues. And he was an active member of the Royal

Philatelic Society, lending them examples from his collection for their exhibitions and becoming the Society's President.

Not long after World War Two it was decided that a book should be compiled:

> '...to present the story of the foundation and development of the Royal Philatelic Collection in a manner worthy of its importance and to record in catalogue form its fascinating and educative contents...'

In 1948 Geoffrey Smith obtained the order to print the book. Clarence Winchester wrote, in its Introduction, that this was not a task to be undertaken lightly, and that it was realised, from the start of the project, that it would need 'considerable forethought and time' if a production worthy of the Collection was to be achieved. In fact some four years and more were to be needed.

Winchester described the close cooperation that was required from all involved and his appreciation of their contribution:

> 'It is proper, therefore, that tribute should be paid to the various artists and craftsmen who...gave without stint and so keenly of their skill...much experiment and not a little patience were demanded of them, and on occasion only time and the finest craftsmanship could solve what seemed to be insurmountable difficulties.'

And difficulties there were aplenty. Besides such problems as finding substitute inks, papers, and processes to accurately reproduce stamps, some of which had been printed nearly a hundred years before, in a variety of materials and by a variety of methods, there was the major issue of security. Obviously the physical conditions necessary for making facsimile of stamps were not present at Buckingham Palace where the stamp albums were kept. This necessitated selected pages from the collection being taken to Ipswich. The fine tuning of the necessary physical environment was sketched out in the journal *British and Colonial Printer* (October 31st 1952):

> 'To achieve minute accuracy of register, stability of the paper and the humidity control system had to be assured, and, by the high quality of the paper, the necessary accuracy was obtained.'

To ensure that the stamps were kept in pristine state they were kept at Cowells for the shortest possible time. Ideally it would have been desirable for the lithographers to actually 'live' with the items they were reproducing, but practically they had to fall back on sometimes using a proof or a reprint impression as a model for retouching (either of which possibly could have had a different appearance from the original).

But brevity of time away from the Palace was not only related to maintaining the physical state of the stamps but also to their value. It was with the greatest secrecy that Sir John and Winchester took selected pages of stamps, worth many thousand of pounds, in their briefcases, across London and on to Ipswich. In one single journey they are reported to have carried one hundred thousand pounds worth of stamps. There is a tale, possibly apocryphal, that one night, the two of them, working late, found there was no safe available in which to lock the stamps, and their solution was to lodge them in a cell at the local police station.

Sir John was to pay many visits to Cowells and charmed those involved in the project with his incredible knowledge of, and enthusiasm for, his subject. They were particularly impressed by his understanding of the various imperfections that had to be reproduced. It was essential for each page to be checked, and checked again, both by Cowell's operatives and by Sir John, who carried out his inspections with a six-time magnifying glass. It was reported that the King died only a few days after he had scrutinised the last proofs.

The Manchester Dispatch (October 23rd 1952) described the stamps as having been reproduced with such unsurpassed accuracy that the impression was that they could be lifted from the page – 'that this is not a book about the Royal stamp collection, but the stamp collection itself'. It is said that at least one stamp, the Mauritius 1847 penny, was a particular concern in this respect, so much so that Cowells was asked to make a small change in the printing to avoid fraud taking place.

Although Winchester declared, in his acknowledgement to contributors to the book, that they were in no particular order, he actually starts with Cowells:

> '...very high praise should be given to Mr. Frederick Fenner and his assistants...for their work on the plates which, it may be conceded, are triumphant examples of facsimile photo-lithographic reproduction. To achieve the high quality essential to this class of work one pair of plates necessitated forty-five colour printings, and such operations were skilfully directed by Mr. Patrick. For so admirably maintaining the close co-operation between the departments concerned I am much indebted to Mr. R. Geoffrey Smith.'

For the book, Smith was the liaison man with author and publisher; Scott the Works Manager; Fred Fenner with Ben Clarke and Bram Wells were manager and operative of the litho department; William Patrick was in charge of the offset and litho printing; Ted Pettitt did most of the colour work; Frank Speller printed most of the monochromes; R.C. Kent and Bob Cooper led the team of compositors; P. Curtis was the proofreader; and F.G. Hall the printers' overseer.

Winchester had set out 'in this age of frustration and difficulty... to show that we can make a Rolls-Royce in books as well as engines'; and this, he, Sir John and Cowells between them achieved. The book was printed in sections, and at intervals, being completed in 1951 to general acclaim.

Subsequently Clarence Winchester edited a further 'royal' volume for the Dropmore Press, again something of a challenge for Cowells. This was *The Crown Jewels and other Regalia in the Tower of London*. It was written by Major-General Lt. D.W. Sitvell, then Keeper of the Jewel House. Winchester was again vainglorious in this introduction to the book claiming that it would 'provide an authoritative and historical document' and that it would 'show and help to maintain British craftsmanship at its best'. As with the King's stamps the printing necessitated a good deal of retouching of photography but for this the visits had obviously to be more from Cowells to check and recheck the colours of the jewels under the watchful eye of the keeper.

1953

THE PLACE OF CROWNING

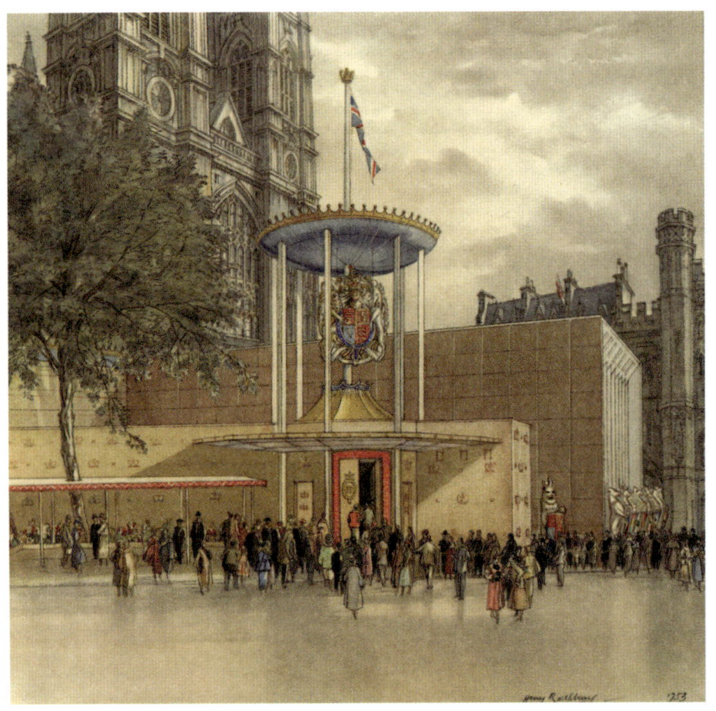

'The Royal Entrance to the Annexe showing the Royal Coat of Arms under the canopy. The Queen's Beasts can be seen on the right outside the main west window'

Cowells printed this beautifully illustrated, if rather curious, book, illustrating the progression of the construction work undertaken by John Mowlem & Co. in preparation for the coronation of Queen Elizabeth. Mowlems had been similarly commissioned for the coronations of Edward VII and George V. They were obviously proud of their royal connections, and no doubt seeing such a publication as useful publicity, were the book's publishers. The subtitle they provided for it explains its contents – 'Its History, Arrangement & Preparation for the Coronation of Her Majesty Queen Elizabeth'.

James Laver was an obvious choice for writing the text. He was, at the time of the Coronation, Keeper of Prints, Drawings and Paintings at the Victoria & Albert Museum, and a prolific writer, particularly on the subject of fashion. In addition he had a passion for stage design and had the Museum's theatre collection under his wing. In that the setting for the Coronation was seen to be a 'stage' the choice of Laver was apt and he threw himself, with some gusto, and not a little pomp, into the history of the coronation ritual and onto a detailed description of Mowlem's work from the initial wrapping of the statuary in Westminster Abbey to the construction of the stands and decorations, not only within the Abbey and in its surroundings, but down the Mall, in Trafalgar Square and along Whitehall.

Laver was appropriately congratulatory of Mowlems efforts:

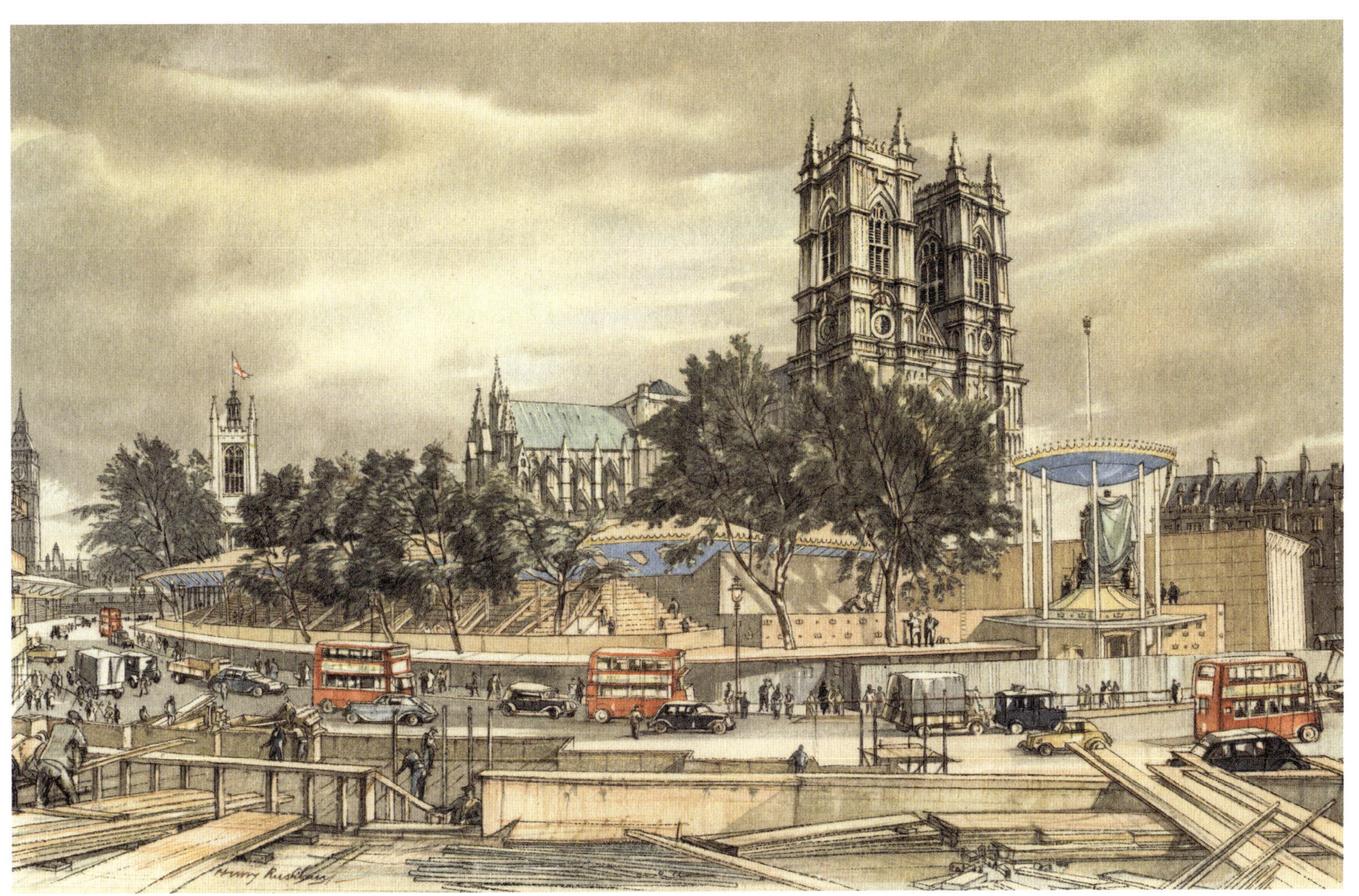

'A view from the stands erected on the site for the new colonial office, showing the Annexe and the stands in front of the Abbey and St. Margaret's, Westminster'

> 'The Public had no awareness of the 500 men employed to bring it about, or the 450 tons of structural steel, the 132,000 cubic feet of timber, the 1,350,000 feet of tubular scaffolding used in the construction…'

and was inclined to the occasional purple passage:

> 'how many must have caught their breath at the sheer beauty of the scene, as the ancient ceremony unrolled itself.'

The illustrations were printed from watercolours by Henry Rushbury (1889-1968). Rushbury was well-known for his topographical views in which the accuracy of his architectural details was softened by his use of colour to produce an appropriate atmospheric effect. He had previously produced some striking reportage, recording such disparate events as a fascist rally in Rome in the 1920s and St. Paul's standing amidst the ruins of Paternoster Row during the bombing in World War Two.

Laver described Rushbury as having a sensitive appreciation of 'works in progress' and wrote that 'he often found a scaffolding erected in the course of construction as exciting as the finished building itself.' Certainly Rushbury's depiction of scaffolding dominates the early illustrations in the book, giving it the grandeur of Gothic pillaring. His ten full page images not only conjure up the challenge Mowlem faced, and the planning and organisation involved, but provide such interesting details as the construction of a railway in the Abbey for the transportation of material. Cowells extraordinary skills with colour, in this instance, display the delicacy of which they were capable when required, albeit their personal preference might lie with bolder work.

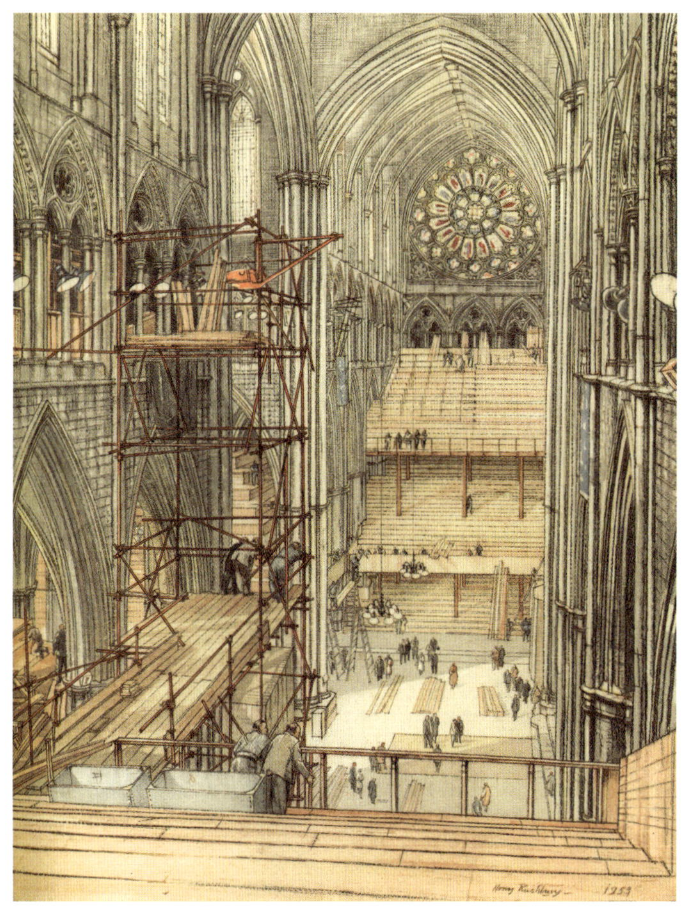

'View of the Peeresses' Gallery in the North Transept. H.M. The Queen is to be seen in the Theatre during one of several visits she made during the course of the preparations'

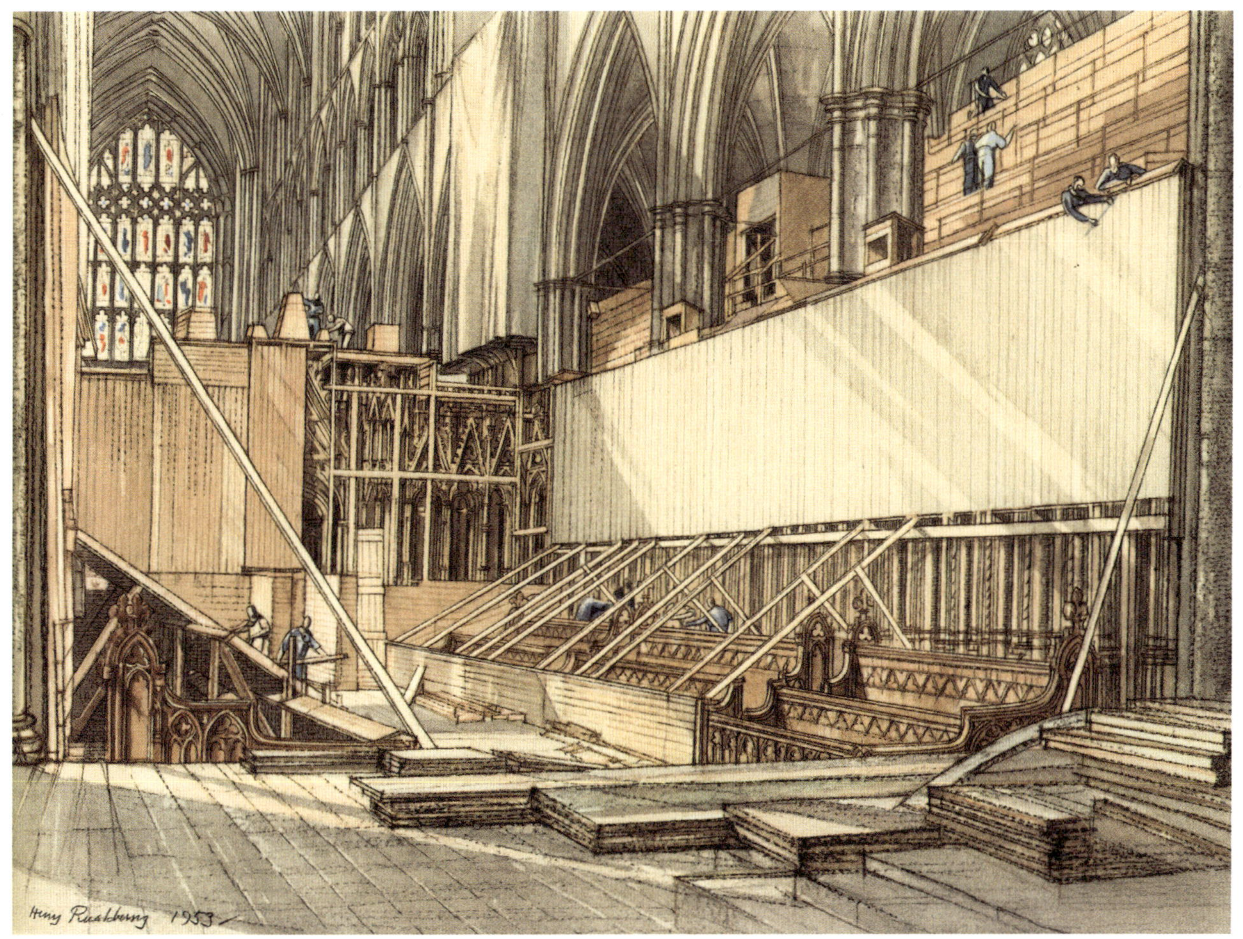

'A view of the Choir stalls and organ loft partly encased in timber to protect them during construction work in the Abbey'

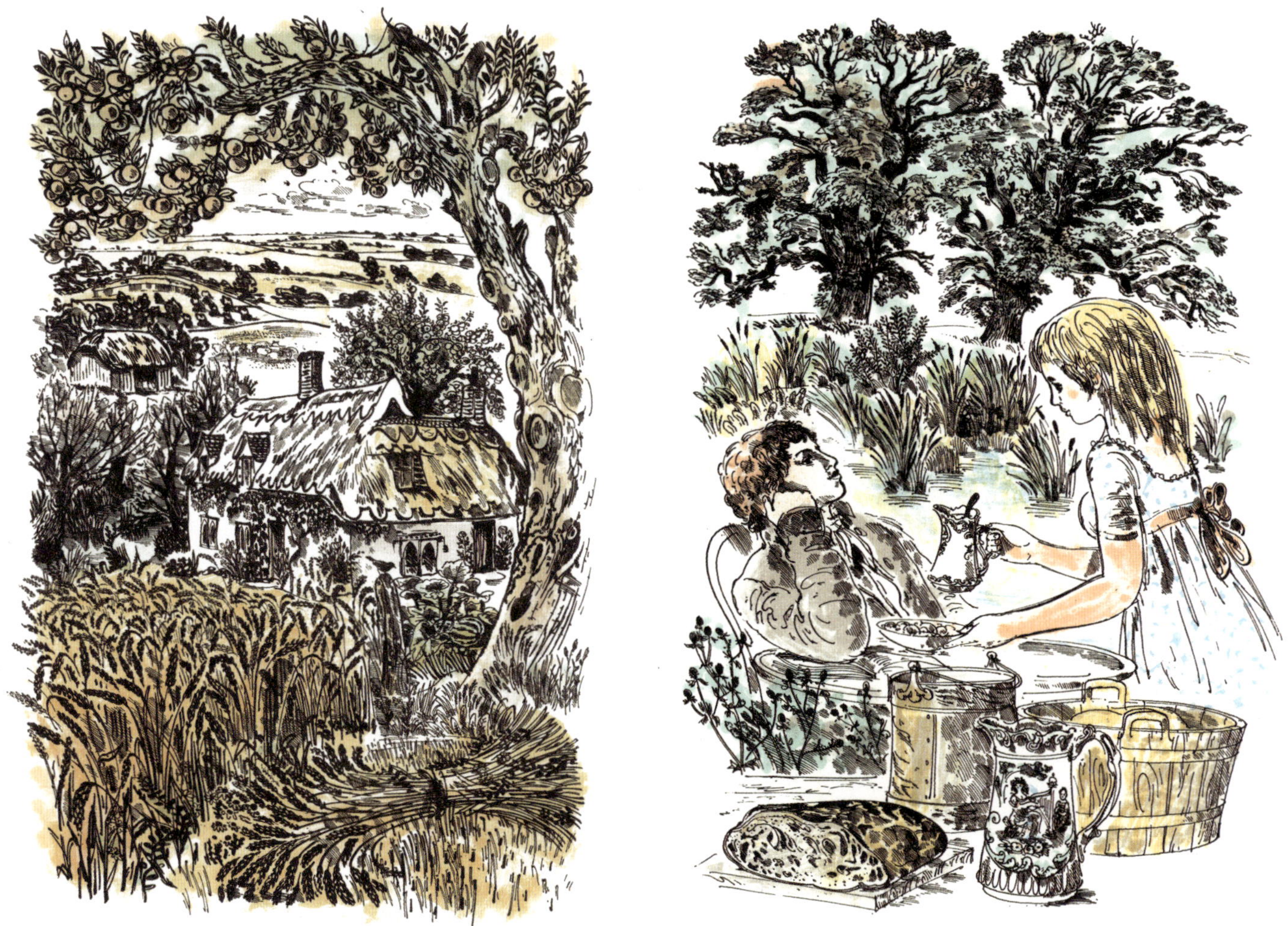

Poems of Keats, *lithographs, 1966*

From 1963

DAVID GENTLEMAN AND THE LIMITED EDITIONS CLUB

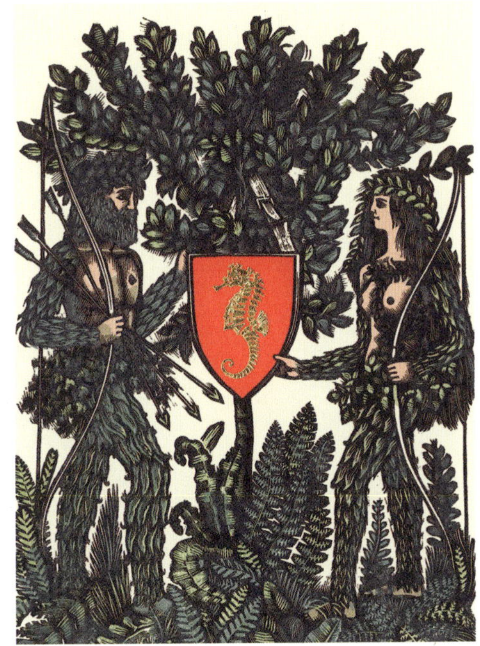

Cowell's Christmas card wood engraving by David Gentleman

One of the most distinguished artists to work with Cowells was David Gentleman, already an established illustrator of repute when he was commissioned to illustrate books for the Limited Editions Club of New York. In fact Gentleman's first contact with Cowells was much earlier, in the 1950s, when John Lewis, by then teaching part-time at the Royal College of Art, took a party of his illustration students on a 'works visit' to Ipswich.

Gentleman's understanding of printing, at that time, would have been the College's letterpress in its printing department and the printing that was going on in Edward La Dell's lithography studio. Not surprisingly he was overwhelmed by the degree of mechanisation he found at Cowells. Curiously he seems to have been as much disturbed by the printer's use of the word 'artwork' as by the machines. With painting as an ambition it had just not occurred to him that the word 'work', with its plebian, earthy, and routine connotations, could be attached to the word 'art', with its heady, creative, near spiritual evocations. Yet, in time, Gentleman came to see the two words as synonymous; that 'art' was the way he intended making his living, and that 'work' could be 'worthwhile, exciting, or even important'.

Indeed it was the 'work' element that seems to have made Gentleman one of the most prolific and productive graphic designers and illustrators of his time. Fiona MacCarthy encapsulated this in her introduction to *The Wood Engravings of David Gentleman*:

> 'He may have sometime balked at his clients' technical demands, or indeed their ideology, but he has welcomed the constraints that commercial work has brought him, believing that working to a brief and to a deadline concentrates the mind.'

Gentleman came so to embrace the notion of 'work' being attached to 'art' that when he came to write a book giving an overview of his own work (to 2002) he actually entitled it 'Artwork'.

Gentleman was to work with Cowells on four books during the 1960s, three commissioned by the Limited Editions Club of New York, and the last by the Imprint Society of Massachusetts. He had just illustrated a charming book – *Bridges on the Backs* – for the designer John Dreyfus, who was a major figure in book design, being typographical adviser to both the Cambridge University Press and to the Monotype Corporation, as well as European consultant to the Limited Editions Club. It was Dreyfus who introduced Gentleman to the Club and to Helen Macy, its formidable owner.

The other key figure for Cowell's Club commissions was Martin Simmons, their agent in New York. Simmons seems to have acted as consultant, wheeler-dealer and even a kind of manipulative puppeteer in his activities as Cowell's agent. In that he may not have been exactly even-handed is suggested in such cynical declarations as:

> 'In my experience if a printer is aware of the extent of a budget he will either be intimidated or unduly mesmerised'.

Simmons, although living in the States for some fifty years, retained his English accent and presented himself as the quintessential

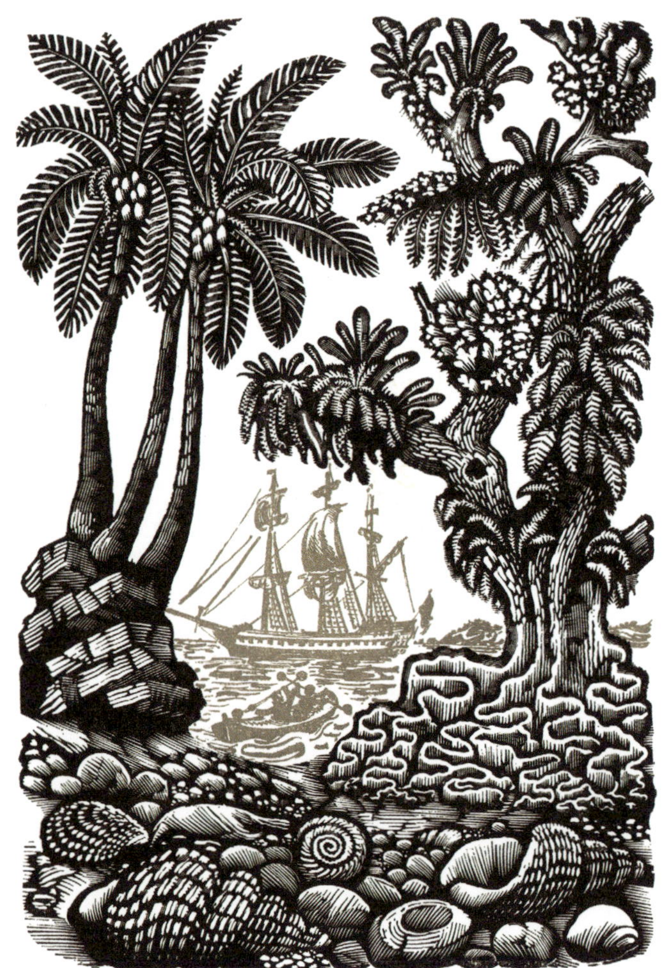

Swiss Family Robinson, *wood engraving, 1963*

Englishman, including a monocle. This appealed to the Americans, who also were to use Cowell's English quaintness in their publicity – the fact that the firm had been started in 1818, and was located in 'the ancient Butter Market'.

In Gentleman's case Simmons appears to have acted as something of a knight at arms, writing to the publishers:

> 'He is an artist of unusual versatility and I suggest the best course of action would be to leave the style of illustration to him...'

Gentleman's first Limited Editions Club book, a tour de force, was *The Swiss Family Robinson* (1963). For this he did twenty-four full-page wood-engravings, with twenty-eight smaller ones appearing in the text, and some forty more as chapter headings. For the other books, printed at Cowells, Gentleman used a combination of pen and ink drawing and water-colour, painted on to Plastocowell. For *The Poems of John Keats* (1966) he produced sixteen full-page illustrations, each requiring up to seven colour separations.

For *The Jungle Book* (1968) Gentleman obtained an Indian government grant, which enabled him to spend some three months travelling in India, with the result that his lithographed colours were altogether bolder and more adventurous. Whilst for *King Solomon's Mines*, for which John Lewis did the typography and book design, Gentleman did twelve colour illustrations (line originals and three colour separations), along with some twenty-four line illustrations of various sizes.

Cowells proffered to Gentleman the same open-minded, co-operative working relationship that had become their hallmark

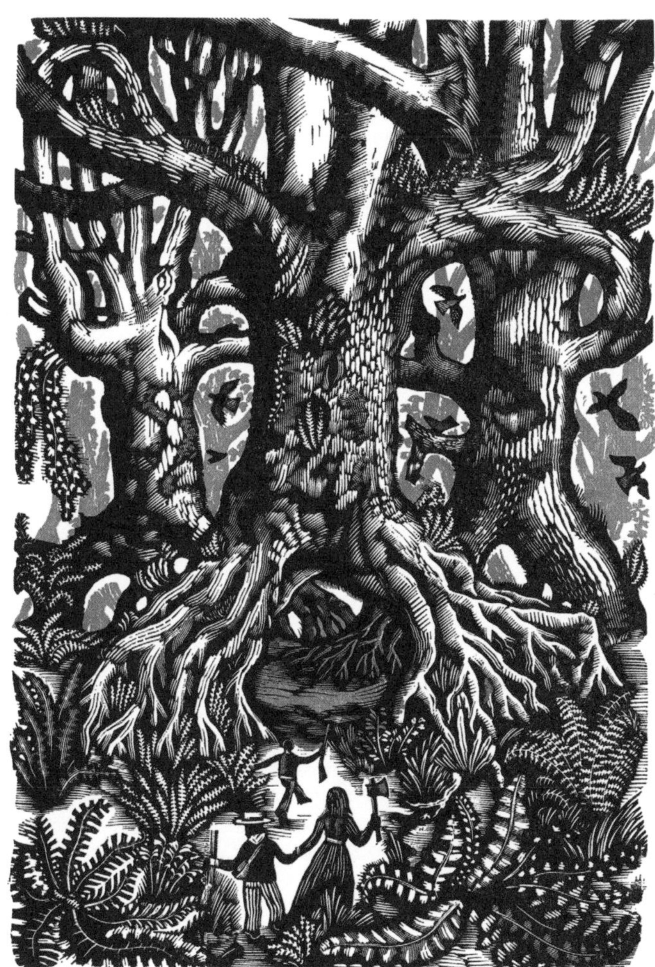

Swiss Family Robinson, *wood engraving, 1963*

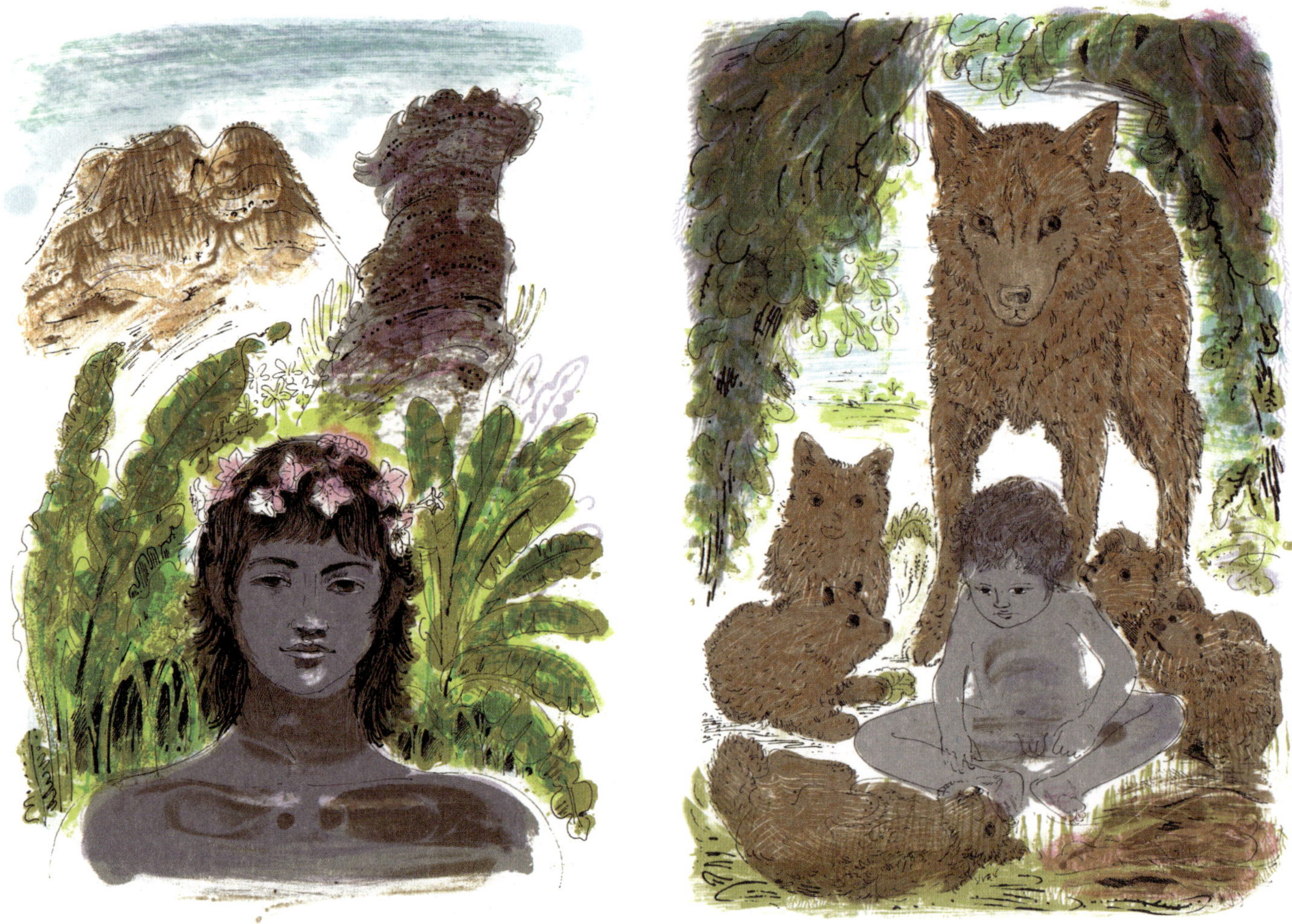

Mowgli *(left) and* Mowgli's Brother *(right), lithographs, 1968*

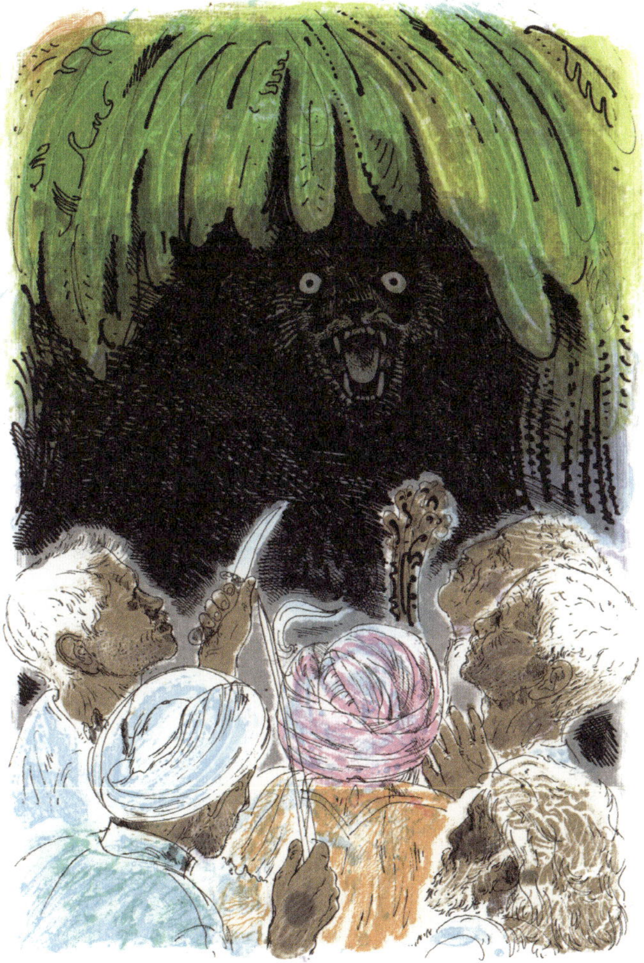

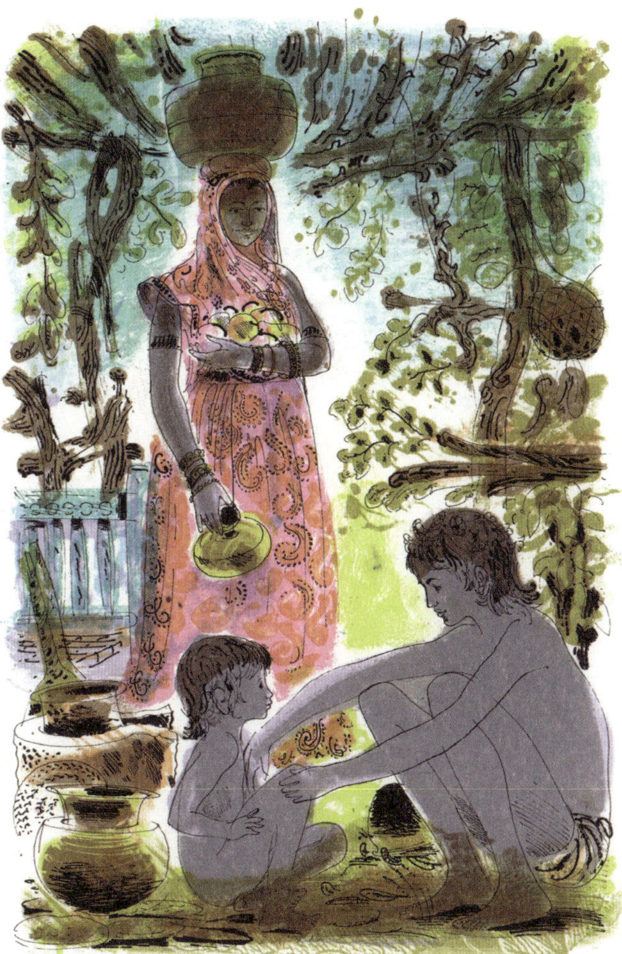

Letting in the Jungle *(left) and* The Spring Running *(right), lithographs, 1968*

when working with artists. They may have been overly keen to promote Plastocowell, but the medium suited Gentleman, who continues, occasionally, to work on plastic to this day. Simmons wrote to the publishers of the onus on Gentleman:

> 'It is possible you will consider Cowell's quotation surprisingly low. If so I should explain that David's working on plastic sheets means that he does a considerable amount of work which otherwise the printer would be doing in making colour separations.'

Correspondence between Gentleman, John Lewis and Cowells on *King Solomon's Mines* illustrates the freedom engendered by the tripartite relationship which enabled Gentleman to say how he wanted to approach the work and for him to give feedback when he felt that Cowells needed to make alterations after proofing. Early on he suggested they use the 'split-duct' in their printing of his illustrations in that he felt it gave a wider colour range and subtlety when only three colours were being employed. And Gentleman suggested a number of other experiments, which Cowells seem to have willingly tried out for him:

> 'If you could print the lightly-exposed plate (therefore more densely-coloured image) in the paler colour, and overprint the other one in the darker, I think that we might get the impression of a very rich depth of reproduction indeed; and this might well be the technique for completing the book altogether.'

Gentleman's work with Cowells not only resulted in four very handsome books (unfortunately with limited distribution in the States and, therefore, now expensive collector's items), but gave him lasting friendships, particularly with Geoffrey Smith, who, as usual, hovered benignly, over all of Gentleman's work with Cowells.

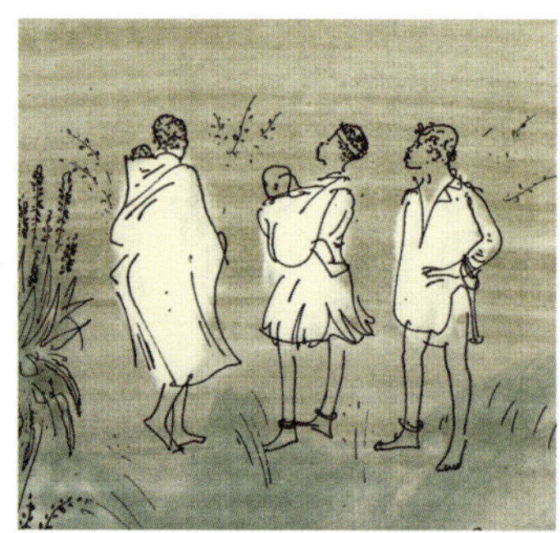

Detail from King Solomon's Mines*, lithographs, 1969*

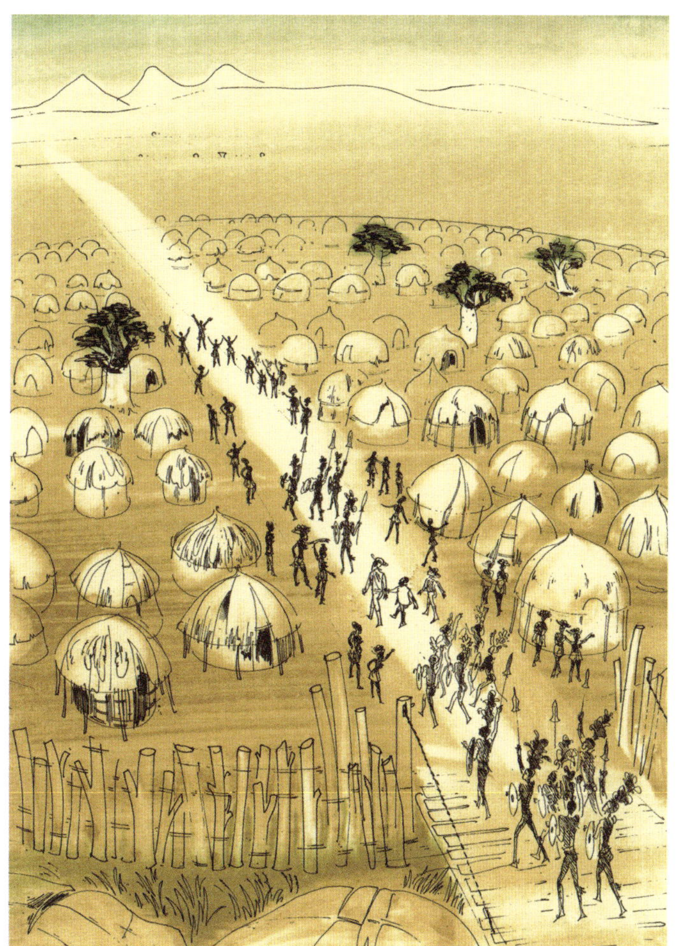

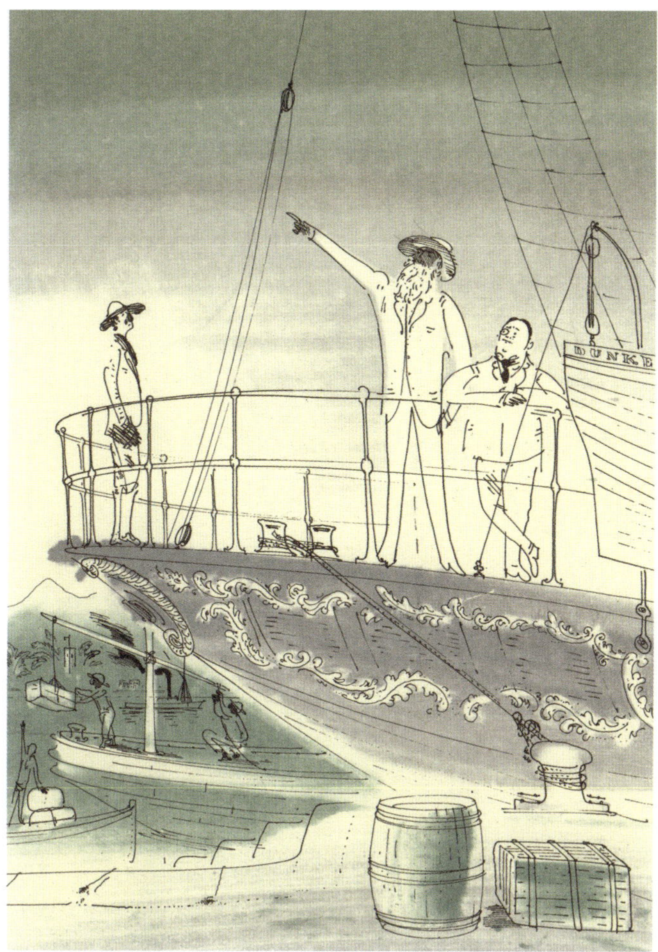

King Solomon's Mines, *lithographs, 1969*

WILD FLOWERS OF THE UNITED STATES

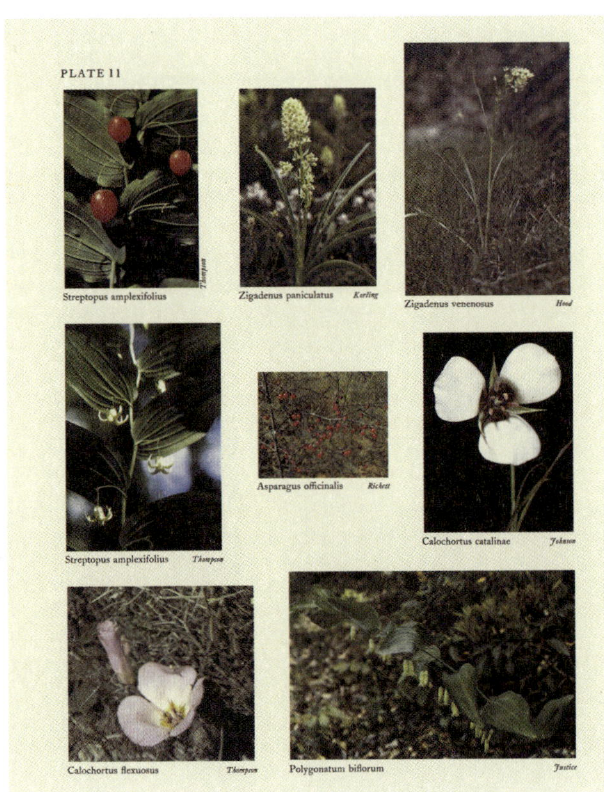

Wild Flowers of The United States

Wild Flowers of The United States was a mammoth undertaking for Cowells, consisting of some six volumes containing fourteen books. The idea for such a book first surfaced around 1956 when Diarmuid C. Russell, an American botanist realised how incomplete the literature on American flora was, and saw the need for a definitive book on the subject. Luckily for him, he had as friends David and Peggy Rockefeller, both enthusiastic plant people, Peggy being on the Board of Managers of the New York Botanical Garden. She was able to convince the Board of the need for such a book, particularly one that was not too technical, fit for the general public, the education of whom was part of the Garden's remit. As the foreword to the first volume put it:

> 'The time seemed ripe to embark upon such an enormous task of making this information available in an interesting and attractive manner, to the intelligent public as well as to other scientists.'

A committee was set up to raise the sum of one million dollars which an initial study had shown to be necessary for collecting the data and presenting it in an accessible way – The National Committee for the *Wild Flowers of The United States* – with Peggy Rockefeller as its Chairman and Russell as the Secretary. When half the funds had been amassed, by 1963, Dr. Harold Rickett was

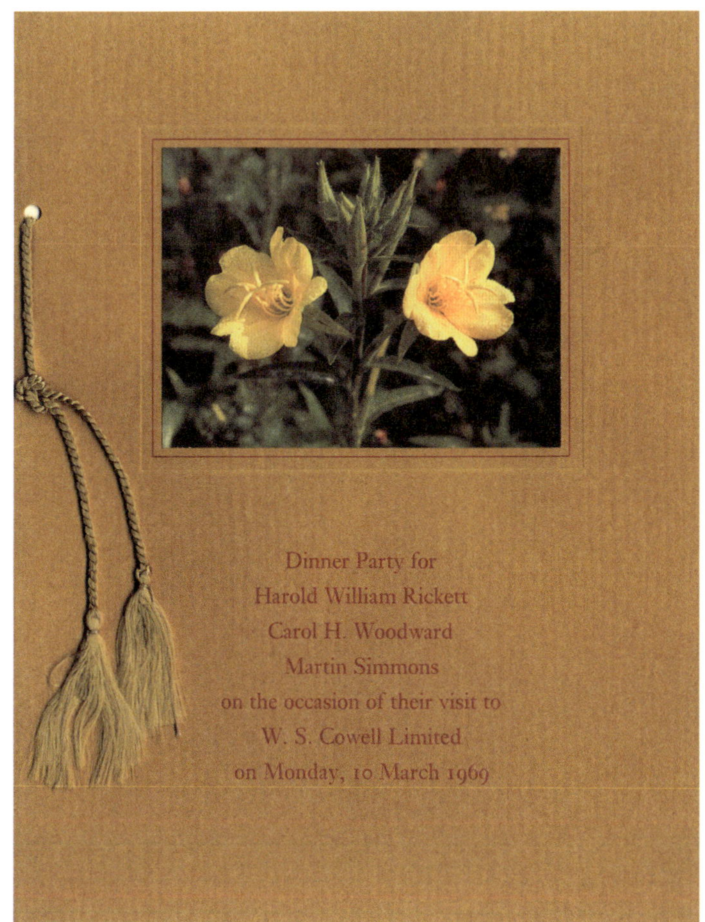

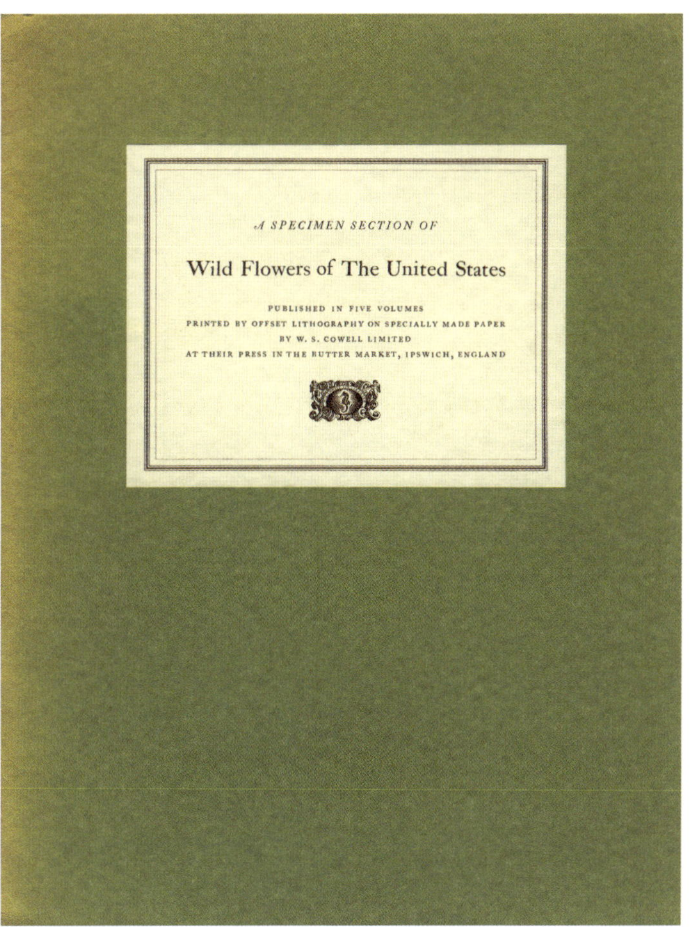

Dinner Party menu for Harold William Rickett, 1969 (left) and
A Specimen Section of Wild Flowers of The United States *(right)*

appointed senior botanist for the project, and William C. Steere commissioned as its overall editor.

Hundreds of people sent in photographs of wild flowers, along with a special group of pictures taken by the nature photographer Charles Johnson, and together these made up the pool from which the final illustrations were chosen; line drawings were supplied by Rachel Speiser.

That Cowells was commissioned to print the book almost certainly came through Martin Simmons. But Smith, who was to be Cowell's link for the project, was quickly on the scene, personally taking the initial trial proofs to the States, while the anxious Cowell printers, cautiously optimistic, awaited New York's judgement on their labours.

The argument for Cowells to be chosen may well have been helped by the fact that they had some history of printing books on botanical subjects. As early as the 1920s they were printers to The Rhododendron Society; and from the late 30s they had worked on some dozen botanical titles, including such curiosities as Stapledon & Davie's *Ley Farming* and Stephen Tallent's *Green Thoughts.*

Although the work was technically difficult the project seems to have had its rewards for those involved. Ricketts was a Yorkshireman, whose family had settled in New York when he was in his teens. He was in his early sixties when *Wild Flowers* was started, yet his visits to Ipswich, two or three times a year to progress the work, seem to have become festive occasions, with much beer drinking and visits to the homes of some of the operatives as well as the directors. Cowells was also visited by Gerry Meyer, production manager for McGraw-Hill, who were publishers for the books, in association with the New York Botanical Garden.

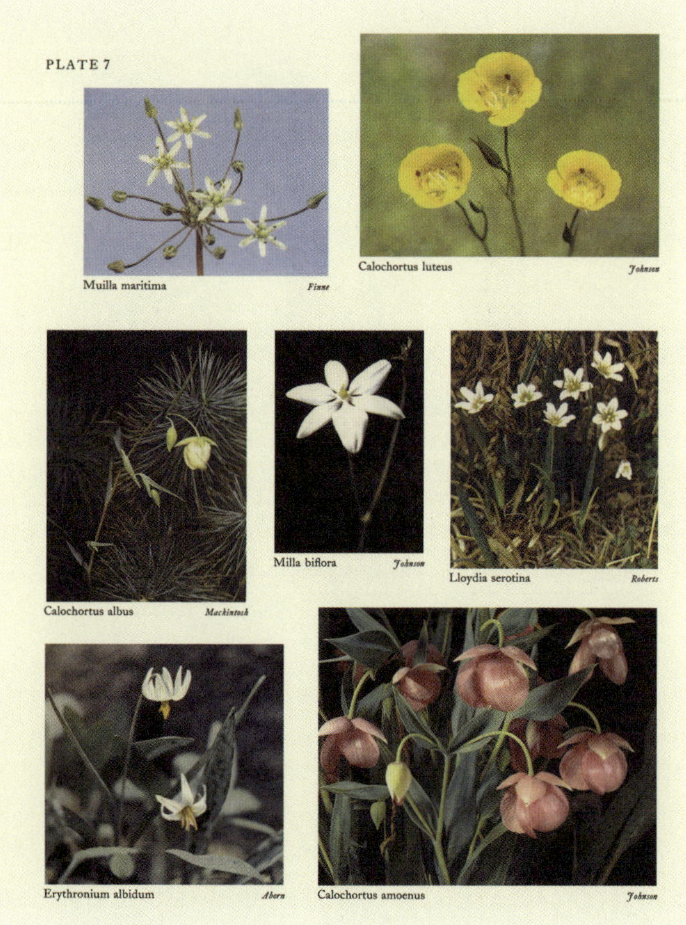

Wild Flowers of The United States

A major technical difficulty with the undertaking was that a number of the flowers to be included bloomed for a very short period in some very remote areas so that often the transparencies that Ricketts brought over with him (some two hundred at a time) were inadequate, certainly when it came to colour. Cowells would frequently have to be on the phone to New York, (without fax or internet), having to rely on a rather inadequate 'colour' vocabulary; much guesswork took place.

A further difficulty was that, certainly during the early stages of the project, Cowells had available only one- and two-colour machines, so that printing sixteen pages at a time, with the continual need to make fine amendments, became a nightmare. Later on a four-colour machine was installed which considerably eased things.

Stanley Colston handled the photographic transparencies coming across with Ricketts, whilst Fred Fenner, and later Ray Limb, supervised the colour reproduction; William Patrick and Bill Ogden oversaw the litho-printing; Maurice Walker did the overall typography and design; and Jim Lomax was responsible for the general administration and progress of the project. Walker and Colston are acknowledged by name on the final page of the final volume. In that the commission took up over seven years of their lives – the first volume being published in 1966, the last in 1973 – the team became personally identified by the work. Stan Colston, for example, saw it as the pinnacle of his life's work and felt completely lost when it was completed. It was he, and Michael Beresford from the Sales office, who went across to New York for the jollities when the final volume came out.

On the strength of *Wild Flowers*, Cowells was further commissioned by the Botanical Garden for two more books, both by Carlyle A. Luer – *The Native Orchids of Florida* (1972) and *The Native Orchids of the United States and Canada* (1975). One commentator, referring to the exceptional standard achieved in the printing of these, ascribed this both to Dr. Luer, whose camera work had found 'that even a gentle zephyr became a gale when a minute subject poses for a portrait', as well as to Cowells who showed 'the highest quality of colour reproduction throughout.' And presumably with the reputation they had got from the first of these, Cowells were retained to print a limited edition volume *Orchidacae* by P. Francis Hunt, which had drawings by Mary A. Grierson and was published by the Bourton Press (1973).

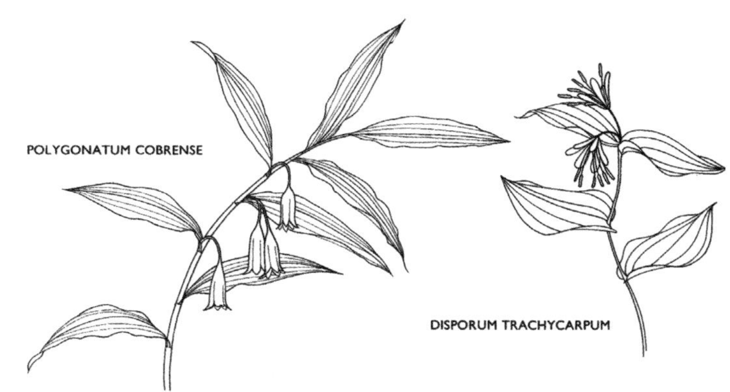

Illustration from Wild Flowers of The United States

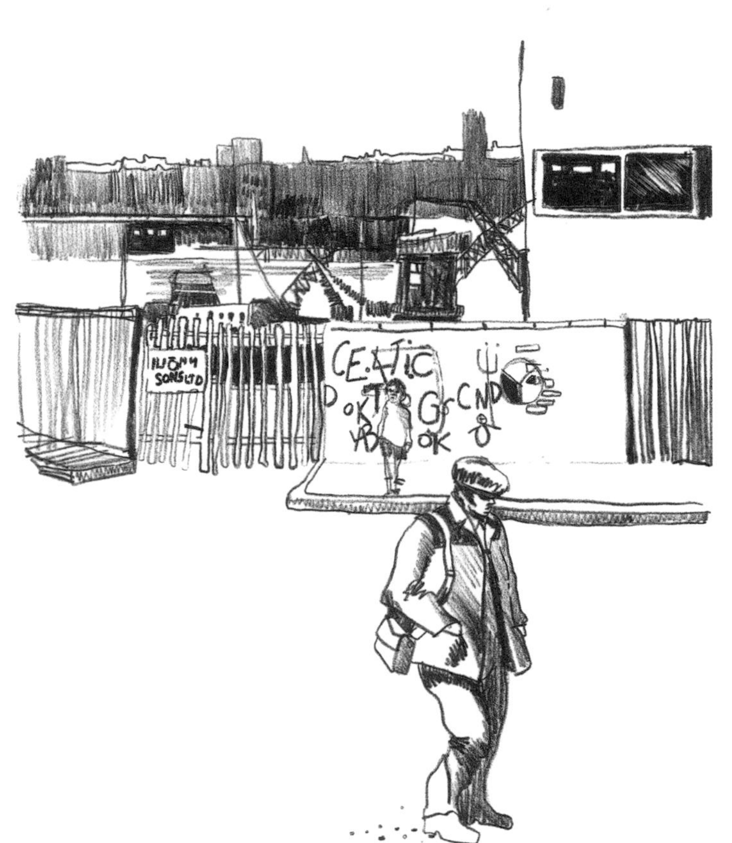

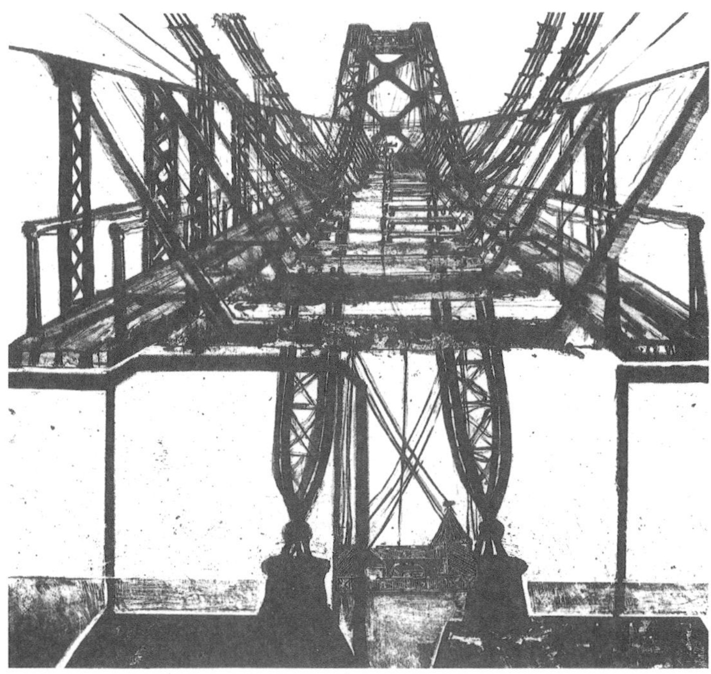

Untitled design by Andy Clark, Glasgow School of Art, 1971 (left),
Transporter Bridge *by Davis (right)*

1970/1971

CHALK MAGAZINE

John Lewis not only retained a working relationship with Cowells after he had moved to the Royal College of Art, acting as a design consultant and having his own books printed there, but in 1970, at his instigation, and with the support of George Scott, Cowells launched a project of liaisons with art colleges. This was to serve two purposes – to further proselytise the use of Plastocowell and to increase Cowell's reputation, by being even further associated with the world of art and design. The actual declared interest was 'to encourage sympathetic working between illustrator and printer.'

The plan was to publish, intermittently, in magazine format, the work of art students from colleges nationwide, each issue to be devoted to one college, the students being given the brief to illustrate anything they chose from the neighbourhood of their college.

The first issue of the magazine, entitled *Chalk,* was undated, but almost certainly came out in 1970. It contained work by selected students from Newport College of Art and Design. In the introduction to *Chalk 1,* Lewis and Scott hint at spreading their concept of 'liaison' beyond art colleges:

> 'This is the first of a series which we at Cowells intend to produce in collaboration with Art Colleges teaching illustration, or groups of artists who specialise in a particular subject.'

And they pointed out that a further spin-off would be that the magazine could be collected by publishers, and other commissioners of illustrators, as a reference file of potential young artists to call upon.

Chalk 2 was introduced a shade smugly:

> 'After the distribution of *Chalk 1* Cowells had a tremendous number of letters from people to whom copies had been sent, giving great encouragement to the project.'

Chalk certainly exposed Colleges to what was, for many of them, a new method of producing prints. Gordon Huntley, then Head of Graphics at Glasgow School of Art, wrote of his College's contribution that he hoped they had managed to demonstrate the versatility of what they had found a rewarding medium. Douglas Halliday, then Head of Graphic Design at Newport was even more enthusiastic about Cowells:

> 'This form of patronage, extended to Colleges of Art by a renowned Printing house, cannot be praised too highly, and we at Newport are extremely grateful for the opportunities it has provided, and wish all success to the venture in the future.'

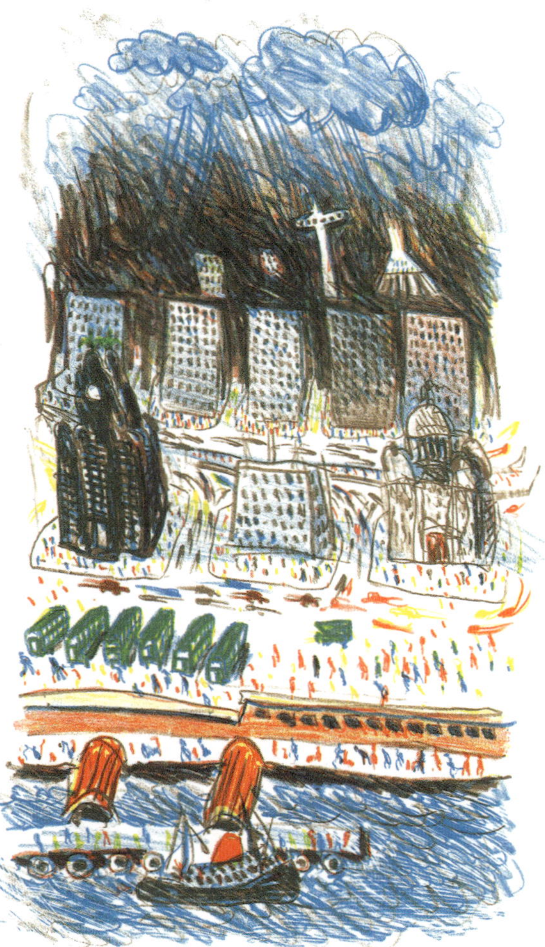

Untitled illustration from Liverpool College of Art issue by Will Rowlands, 1970

In fact, only four issues of *Chalk* appeared for Newport, Liverpool, Glasgow and Coventry (Lanchester) Colleges of Art. It is not clear why the project was not extended. But, as with many similar schemes, much depended upon the continued energies and enthusiasm of the originators and certainly all was not going well at Cowells by then.

Nevertheless in the four issues that were published, the students' offerings give an interesting insight into their street-wise preoccupations at the beginning of the 70s – the underdog (tramps, minorities, the aged, the work-worn), and the decline of their environment (graffiti, pollution and run-down factories). Where colour was used it tended to be brash and with a posterlike 'in-your-face' effect. Yet there are a number of examples where students have shown a quick and sensitive response to what was around them, using their new experimenting with Plastocowell. Particularly haunting were Grahame Ward's *The urban reality – pollution* and the angst of Robin Harris's untitled adolescent girl looking on to a dreamlike scene in a Liverpool street.

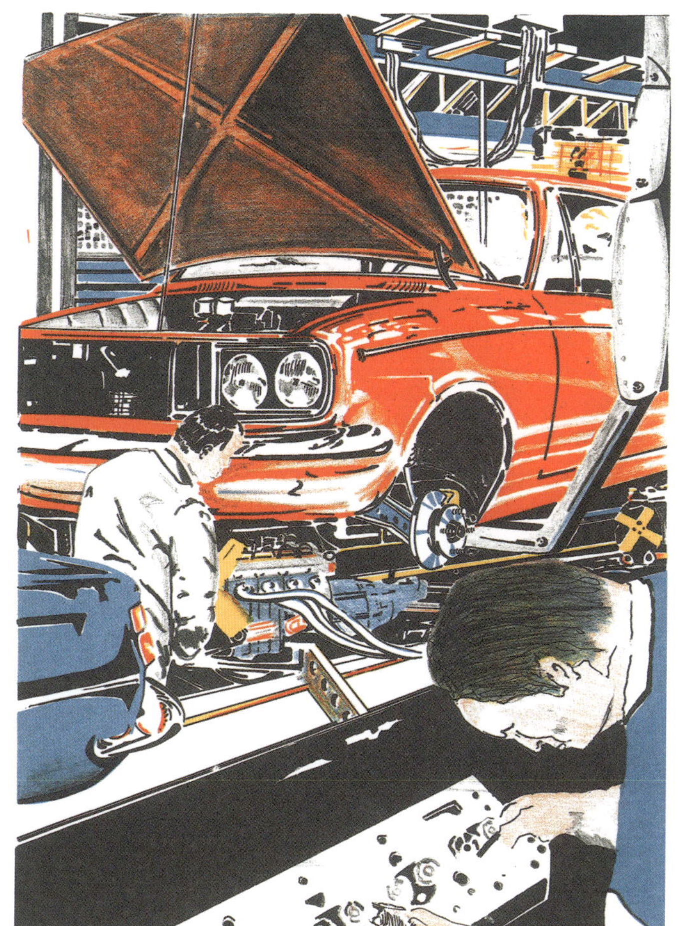

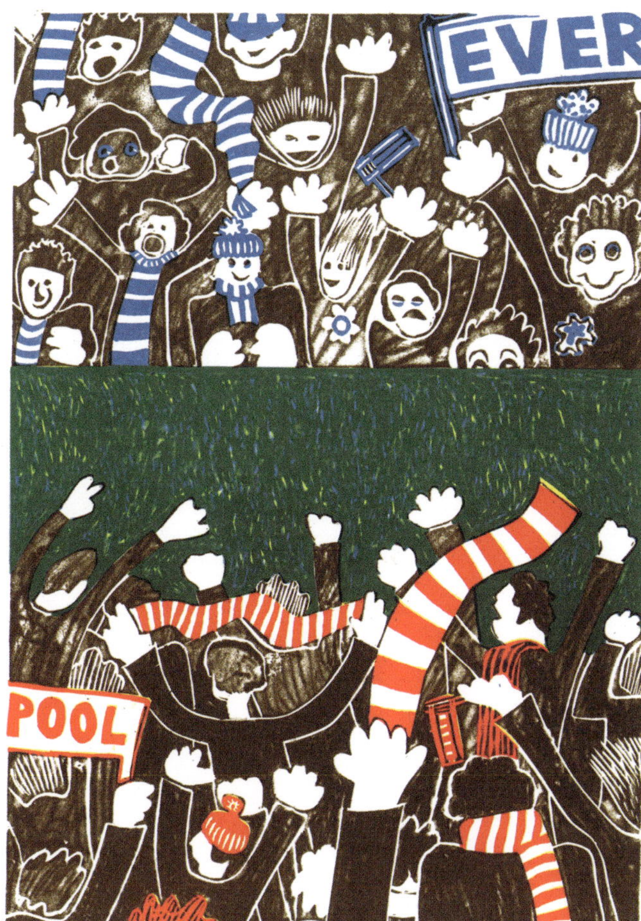

The Assembly Line *by Derek Alexander from the Coventry College of Art issue, 1971 (left) and page from the Liverpool College of Art issue (right)*

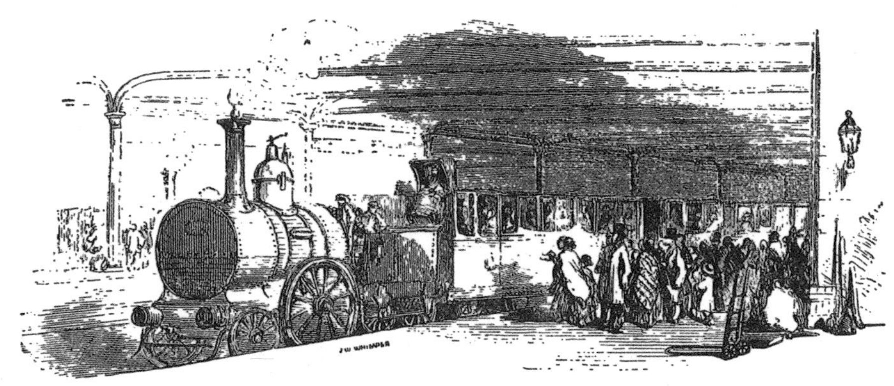

OUR STARTING TRAIN.

FROM BISHOPSGATE TO IPSWICH IN 1851

EPILOGUE

In his address given at Stationer's Hall, London in 1959, Professor G.A. Ovink, the renowned Dutch typographic designer, spoke on 'Fitting Design into Hard Business'. He, like Geoffrey Smith, was concerned about relationships in publishing and printing:

> 'In all industrial arts, including printing, the key to work quality is harmonious co-operation on a basis of mutual understanding between the three main interests concerned – the salesman, the technician and the artist.'

Ovink was perhaps remiss in not including the author, the writer of the text, in his 'harmonious team'. He was optimistic that all involved could work productively together in spite of their being possibly psychologically and sociologically different, and almost certainly having different, albeit overlapping, motivations. He appreciated what the likes of Ruskin, Morris, Ashbee, Letheby, and Gill were seeking with their concepts of guilds, workshops and communities, and felt that a mechanised factory, working within such constraints as employers and artists codes of conduct, trade union regulations and attitudes, price regulations and tariffs etc. could nevertheless work towards something similar. He was convinced that if sales and technical people could appreciate that design was not an afterthought but was central to commercial success and to building the reputations of all involved, (not just that of the designer), then with clever selling, efficient production and good design everybody could emerge from a project feeling O.K.

> Ovink concluded with:
>
> 'This co-operative spirit (of mediaeval printers) did not reach the level of ordinary printing until the development of Monotype in Europe and the influence, for instance of the Nonesuch Press; and after the Second World War, of Lund Humphries through the Penrose Annual, of the Curwen Press, the Shenval Press and Cowells...'

Ovink elevated Cowells to the Pantheon of the time; and, although it may be a shade pretentious, Smith, Hanson and Scott were a kind of triumphal triumvirate, proving themselves to be an interesting example of one of Ovink's 'harmonious teams', at least during the halcyon days of W.S. Cowell Ltd.

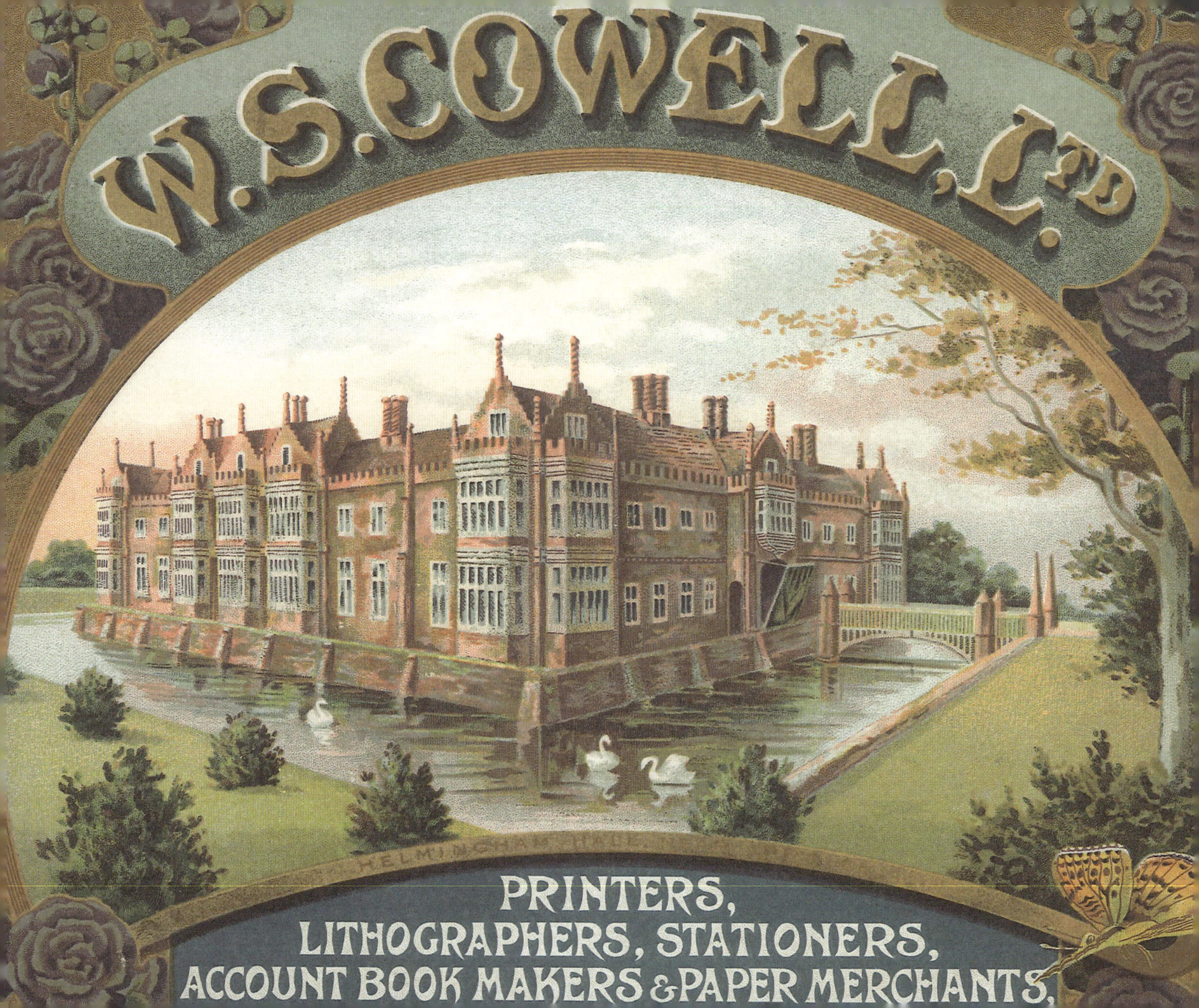

W. S. COWELL, LTD.
HELMINGHAM HALL
PRINTERS,
LITHOGRAPHERS, STATIONERS,
ACCOUNT BOOK MAKERS & PAPER MERCHANTS,

BIBLIOGRAPHY

1952 Edward Ardizzone 'A Simple Technique in Line and Colour Wash' Penrose Annual

1957 Noel Carrington 'A Century of Puffin Picture Books' Penrose Annual

1959 G.W. Ovink 'Fitting Design into Hard Business' Wynkyn de Worde Society

1960 Geoffrey Ireland 'The Press in the Butter Market' W.S. Cowell Ltd.

1967 John Lewis 'The Twentieth Century Book' Studio Vista

1974 George Scott 'Foundations of Quality' W.S. Cowell Ltd.

1992 Ian Rogerson 'Noel Carrington & His Puffin Picture Books' Manchester Polytechnic Library

1994 John Lewis 'Such Things Happen' Unicorn Press

1994 Kathleen Hale 'A Slender Reputation' Frederick Warne

2003 Brian Alderson 'Edward Ardizzone, a Bibliographic Commentary' Oak Knoll

2006 Ruth Artmonsky 'The School Prints, a Romantic Project' Artmonsky Arts

2010 Joe Pearson 'Drawn Direct to the Plate' Penguin Collectors Society

The W.S. Cowell Ltd. Archives are held at the Suffolk Record Office, Ipswich
The Puffin Picture Books Archive is in the Penguin Archives, Special Collections, University of Bristol

From The Penrose Annual, 1949, by Geoffrey Smith

AUTOLITHOGRAPHIC PROGRESS AND PLASTIC FILM

A lithograph provides the simplest medium for an artist to reproduce his own design directly. There is no need for him to make a finished drawing to reproduce by one of the photographic methods, or for a lithographic artist or copyist to translate his ideas. The artist may work on stone in one or more colours, on a grained metal plate, or on transfer paper.

There is another surface he can use – plastic film, to which I shall refer later.

Autolithography is a term used to describe the several techniques through which the artist creates his own lithograph. Often he does not reproduce. There is really no need for him to make a finished sketch – he can create his lithograph step by step and colour by colour. This seems to be the keynote of the success of autolithography. He knows the results he wants, knows the limitations of the process, and, continually learning as he goes along, often achieves the result he requires – or rather the feeling he wants to convey – without having to compromise.

A lithographic draughtsman is trained to aim at facsimile, and any form of compromise is dangerous. He cannot achieve facsimile without an undue number of colours – prodigal both of time and expense. His compromise may well be in the opposite direction to the kind of compromise acceptable to the artist who made the drawing, and thus the result is not so satisfactory.

I am not suggesting for one moment that the author artist will supplant the litho artist or draughtsman. There will always be plenty of work for him.

The direct work of artist has revived interest in drawn lithography generally, as distinct from photolithograph, and this field includes book, jackets, wallcharts, ad posters which are being reproduced in the printer's works in considerable numbers. Many printers who are interested in the progress of the lithographic process feel that this is an encouraging sign.

Autholithograhy has been gaining in popularity for book illustration for a number of years and great impetus was given to the work when, in 1940, Allen Lane launched the Puffin Picture Books, which have been a great success. Due to the method of production these children's books have given better value than ever before, not only from the design point of view, but in many cases from the reproduction standard. Two of the titles which call for special comment are *Town and Village* and *Trees in Britain*, both by S.R. Badmin. The standard of these books has been recognised by inclusion among books specially selected for exhibition in many countries. It seems that this series has stimulated other publishers to use autolithography for books and for prints. The range is wide, including limited editions of expensive volumes as well as mass production.

A number of artists who names are widely known, as well as younger ones, are taking up autolithography on stone or plate. The trade welcomes this because the more artists who understand the lithographic process, the better it is for the reproducer and printer.

It has been the policy of the editor of the *Penrose Annual* to encourage greater co-operation between artists and lithographers and printers' publishers and production managers. This is an idea I heartily endorse. Considerable advances have been made, but much remains to be done. If every artist, whether he be autolithographer or working for reproduction, were to spend just one day (or far better, two consecutive days) at a lithographic works, the quality of reproduction would rise immeasurably. Many artists could testify to this. Lithographic firms are far readier to co-operate and provide the facilities than they were before the war.

It is encouraging to find that the art schools are taking more and more interest in lithography. Some names that come to mind are the Ruskin School of Painting, Oxford, Chelsea Art School, the Central School of Arts and Crafts, Camberwell School of Art, Kingston School of Art, and those at Bristol, Reading, Croydon, Hammersmith, Sheffield, Guildford, and other centres. It is hoped these schools are in close touch with the lithographic printers nearby for advice and possibly spare equipment, since the available plant in many Art Schools and Colleges who teach lithography leaves much to be desired. There is a great difference in the atmosphere in a school and a printing 'shop'; in the classroom atmosphere artists often do not capture sufficient enthusiasm to progress as far as they might, and remain unaware of many of the possibilities of the process.

Many publishers have paid for their designers and illustrators to visit printers, but it is noteworthy that few production managers of advertising agencies send their staff or even trouble themselves to become familiar in a practical way with the facilities lithography offers and the techniques used.

A very fine series of pictures, many of them autolithographic, but all of them drawn on plates, were produced in 1947 by Chromoworks Ltd., under the supervision of Barnett Freedman, for Messrs J. Lyons & Co. Ltd. for showing in their teashops and restaurants. Messrs. Lyons are to be congratulated for their enterprise and the wide encouragement such a scheme gives.

During the war an excellent series of pictures for the decoration of messes, wardrooms, canteens, etc., was produced by the Arts Council, or C.E.M.A. as it was then. More recently the Travel Association have distributed posters by well-known artists. Not all the latter were drawn lithographically, but to get the best results this method was chosen for several of them.

School Prints Ltd., who publish autolithographs exclusively, have shown enterprise in producing a very interesting and attractive range for distribution through the schools and elsewhere.

Several publishers have schemes in hand for wallcharts for schools, as well as the improvement of their long-established series of educational books, by the introduction of colour lithography.

Skilled lithographic artists, as such, have not been standing

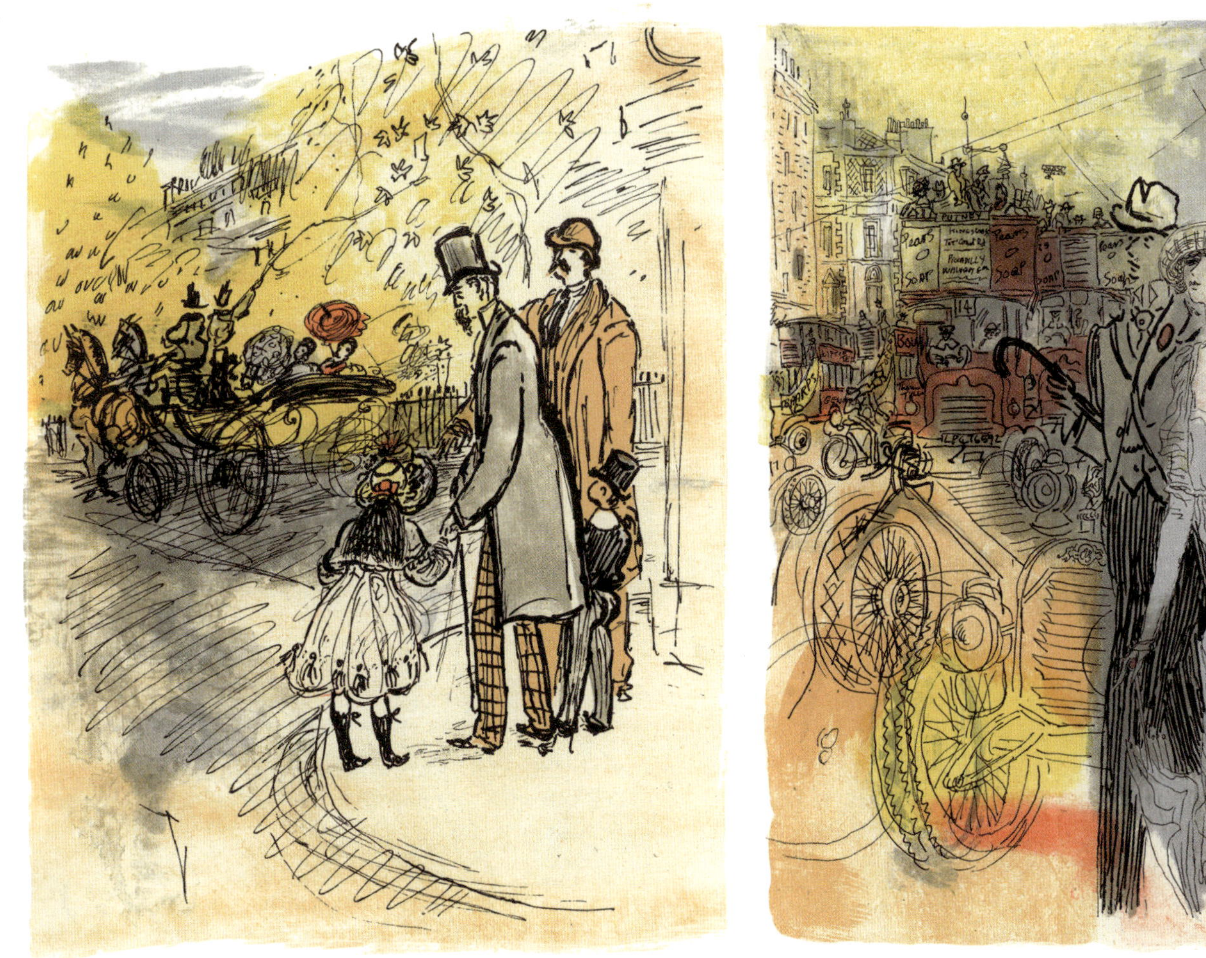

Illustrations to Galsworthy's Forsyte Saga *published by William Heinemann…*

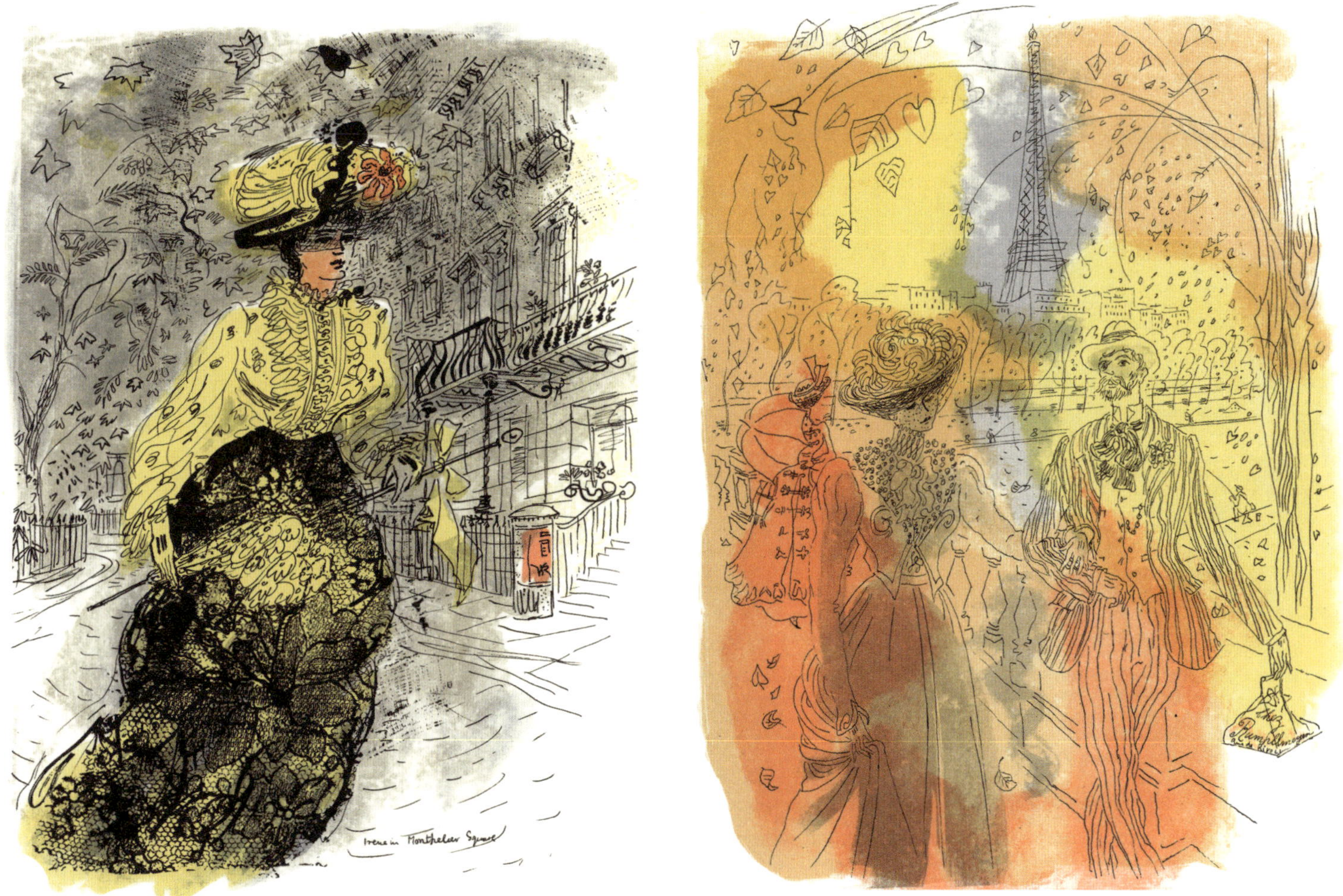

...drawn on Plastocowell by Anthony Gross. Printed by W.S. Cowell

still, and intelligent interpretation of drawn lithography of artists' originals has been developing on new lines; T.E. Griffits, who wrote on their subject in the *Penrose Annual* in 1940 Vol. 41, has continued his good work and encouraged others to follow on similar lines. In a recent lecture to the Association of Teachers in Printing and Allied Subjects, he said: 'The old-established method of drawing and printing the light colours first, and then building up with darker ones is giving place to an easier, quicker, and better method of drawing. The darker colours are drawn and printed first, the highlights filled in with the lighter colours, the darker colours being subdued with the semi-opaque colours. Texture is less visible, and less time is taken in chalking tints by using more realistic use of the medium in the manner very similar to oil painting, or opaque watercolours, or pastel.'

I recently saw an autholithograph, *Cargo Ships in Sete*, by G. Couderc, which is produced in this way. In this case the black was printed first, then a pink and a light blue, each with white added, both colours being overprinted onto portions of solid black to reduce the depth of black to a warm or cold dark grey. After this a chrome yellow, which made some definite drawing at the top black portion of the ship on the picture and which was also used over the pink to produce some browns and oranges. The next colour was red, and finally a semi-transparent royal blue was used, this last printing deepening the black in parts, and on the light blue, where it had subdued the black, it produced a very rich, deep blue. The whole thing showed absence of texture to a marked degree.

Several artists, to avoid using cumbersome lithographic stones, or the less cumbersome but still heavy zinc plates, draw on transfer paper, making use of the well-known Pennell paper. This method is, I believe, in favour with many members of the Senefelder Club, being, until now, the only easily transportable material, thus enabling sketches to be made on the spot, where stone or plate would be impracticable. This process has another advantage over stone or plate in that the proofing man does put the actual artist's work from the Pennell paper onto the printing plate instead of first 'pulling' his transfer from the stone or plate, so that one possible source of depreciation in quality is saved, always providing the picture has not to be reversed. But, on the other hand, there is no original to fall back on if the putting down of the Pennell paper is not satisfactory.

The latest development in autholithography is a new plastic material or film in place of stone of plate, the importance of which it seems at moment, difficult to access. It is used with equal success for black and white or for colours. The range of techniques which can be employed seems unlimited. Any number of colour plates can be prepared from a key drawing without any drawing on the film are preferably offset deep, thus preserving meticulously accurate reproduction for large editions of hitherto short-lived techniques. New plates of equal quality can be made at any time. There is no middle process such as transferring, between the artist's original and the machine plate; it must be realised that even the best transferred plate cannot be so faithful in quality as the plate made by plastic technique.

The originals can be used for the production of line blocks, again yielding results in line work hitherto impossible.

The material used is specially prepared, thin-grained plastic, non-stretching material. Opacity of the work on the original is a *sine qua non*, so the medium used for solid or line work is spotting medium, and for chalk work a chinagraph pencil. While these are by no means perfect media, there are many there which can be used, but they have attendant drawbacks. The two mentioned have the advantage of permitting erasures for alterations.

Brushes, pens, engraving tools, air brushes, darning needles, a pocket knife, in fact almost anything to produce a variety in texture can be used. A constant check on the opacity of the drawing is necessary, and for this purpose a 'light' table is really necessary so that the drawing may be examined as the work proceeds by *transmitted light*; a magnifying glass is also a great help.

The artist must draw the design as in lithographic reverse, or as seen in a mirror. While this may be a disadvantage in the case of black and white, it is immaterial in colour work provided there is a key, as this key can be reproduced in non-photographic light blue on reverse of the plastic, so that the subsequent colour drawing is the correct way round for the printer.

This process should hasten a return to books being copiously illustrated in black and white, as it is arriving in the midst of similar developments in reproduction of type and the printing of books by photolithography, and also the development of photo-composing machines.

I visualise artists roaming the country with sketch books of plastic material instead of paper. It will introduce more pleasing techniques into newspaper line blocks. For certain types of pictures the use of plastic film will challenge the hitherto acknowledged supremacy of collotype for best work, with its limited quantities and inconsistency. Indeed, the possibilities of plastic have quickly been recognised. Next year pictures executed by a number of modern French artists, headed by Picasso and Matisse, using this plastic method will be available.

Altogether a very exciting development, of which at present only the fringe has been explored.

From The Penrose Annual, 1950, by Noel Carrington

AUTOLITHOGRAPHY OF PLASTIC PLATES

The use of transparent plate, instead of stone or zinc for original drawings in lithographic printing, seems to have been developed first in Germany. As so commonly happens in the affairs of men, it was the needs of war that supplied the spur of experiment. The map making department of the German Army wanted a means of turning out cheap and rapid editions of maps for special purposes on a campaign. For such maps colour printing and good register are as important as speed. Two or three years before the war the Dynamit firm in Troisdorf, near Cologne, had produced the original astrolon, which had the required qualities – lateral stability and an even grain. In 1946 the Enschede firm at Harleem were using I.C.I. Perspex with satisfactory results, and I believe the technique had been brought by the Germans to Holland during the war. The plates were being grained in the same machine as that used for graining metal, but they were being rather heavy gauge for use by artists. The thinner the plastic sheet the clearer the register the artist can obtain, but it is, of course, absolutely essential that there should be no shrinkage or stretch at any later stage if accuracy of register is to be maintained throughout the job. The lack of these qualities has sometimes led to disastrous results when celluloid materials were used. A plate which will answer the most exacting requirements has now been produced in this country, for which printers (and indeed, artists too) have to thank Messrs. W.S. Cowell of Ipswich. This firm has shown great initiative in the matter. The researches carried through at Ipswich are of the character ordinarily assumed by research in states with independent funds.

In this article it is with the autolithographic use of the plastic plate artists that I am chiefly concerned, and its other very important technical potentialities must be dealt with elsewhere. It seems likely that the plastic plate will completely replace the metal plate as an original plate on which the artist works. There are artists who are faithful to the stone and if it serves them well their faith is natural and justified. The zinc plate had for some years been used as a substitute for stone, largely because of its comparative lightness in weight. Certainly it was inferior to the stone as a medium for draughtsmanship, and transfer from one metal plate to another was the most uncertain factor in the whole process. Although artists of insufficient experience were often to blame for overworking – or underworking – their original plate, nevertheless the deterioration that could be detected between the proofs from artist's plate and machine plate was sufficient to make many artists forswear the process for good and all. This deterioration increased usually with each transfer from the master plate, so that though it was there in safe keeping as a master, it soon became a very damaged 'old master' that nobody could be proud to resuscitate. I have on various occasions questioned litho experts as to the number in quality. The answers varied from 'a dozen' or 'a hundred' – it being emphasised always that this was dependent naturally on the skill of the craftsman making the transfers. I must state, however, that rather bitter experience suggests that for only a few transfers is the freshness of the original obtained. This did not apply to transfers from the stone.

The plastic plate enjoys several distinct advantages over the metal. In the first place its tone, placed as it can be over white paper or an artificially lit screen, is much less exhausting to the eye than the dull grey of the zinc. Erasions are not difficult and engraving is a feasible alternative to the pen line. It is just as suitable for chalk, and experiments seem to show that a tone derived from thin wash will reproduce accurately and with a good texture. Apart from this, the transparent nature of the plate enables register to be kept throughout the job where many plates are needed for colour printing. Offsets of a key drawing can be printed down on the plastic in exactly the same way as it is customary to print them down on zinc guides. When the original plate is complete a contract negative is made into a photographic plate, and this forms the permanent basis for making the machine, but the original plastic plate remains undamaged and can be worked on again should it prove desirable. That the plastic is a point which will not be missed by printing houses with experience of the two.

I have discussed the merits of the two plates with many artists who have had considerable experience of both. They all agree that the plastic is better from their point of view, not only because it is easier on the eye and to handle, but because the final printing is closer to their intention. It is necessary to master one thing; that is the density of chalking on the plate through which the light will come when a contact negative is made. A few experiments seem sufficient for most artists. Some find that to work on a sloping glass screen with a diffused light underneath is preferable to laying the plastic over white paper. Messrs. Cowell have permitted a score of artists to try their hand on the plates in order that the whole range of possibilities can be explored. Some of these proofs which I have been privileged to see are distinctly exciting. They suggest that as a medium for prints the plastic plate will soon be as important as stone, copper or wood. It is perhaps unfortunate that the famous French artists who were persuaded to draw prints on plastic for School Prints Ltd. did not seem to take any great pains to develop the advantages inherent in the new plates, though it is perhaps rash to judge without knowing their exact intentions. It is obviously too early to assess the final place that plastic plate will hold in relation to the older medium. A good deal in the way of experiment still needs to be done. In this connexion it is rather interesting to note that one of the first uses of the plate by artists was in an ambitious project fathered by the Directors of the Amsterdam City Museum in 1945. It was carried out by a co-operative sales organisation of young Dutch artists, anxious to bring their work within everyone's financial reach. The well-known firm of Van Leer and Company in Amsterdam also co-operated in this scheme, which was highly successful.

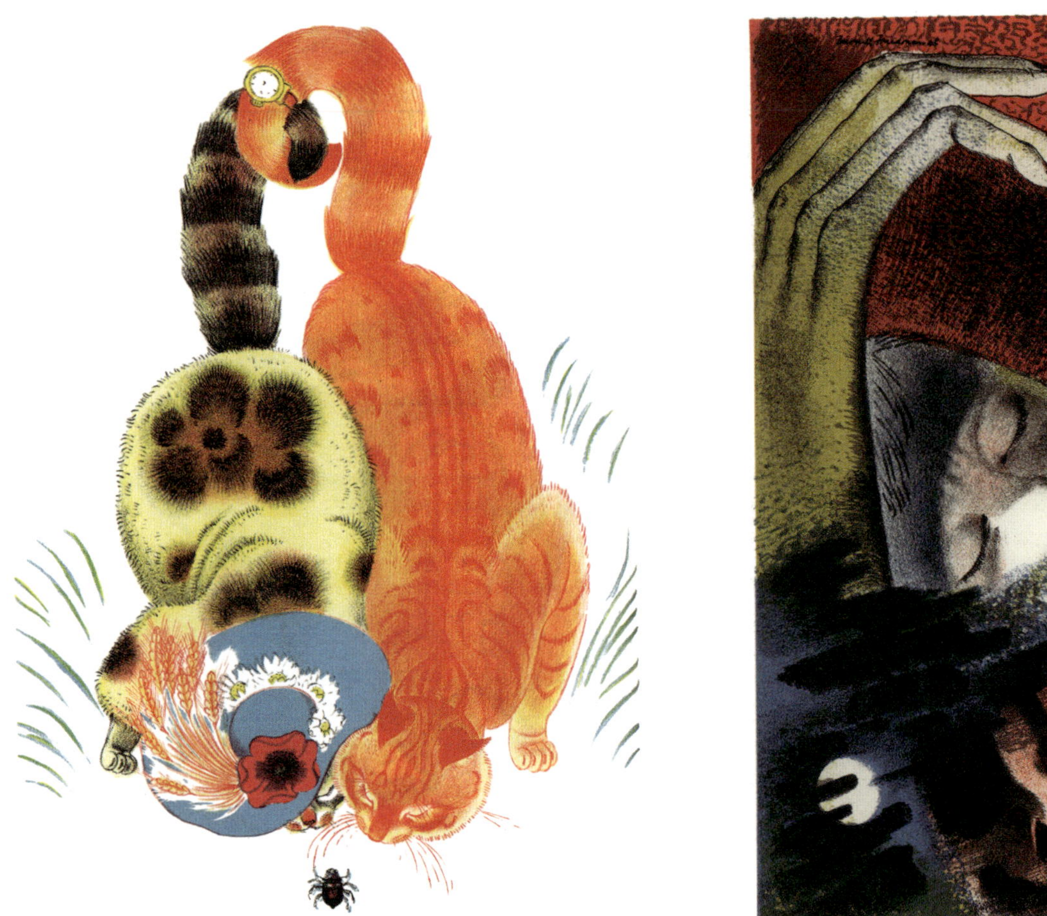

Illustration from Orlando Buys a Dog *by Kathleen Hale (left), lithograph drawn on the stone by Barnett Freedman for a* Handbook of Printing Types *(right), both printed by W.S. Cowell Ltd.*

In book illustration the plastic plate has already justified itself. In the Puffin *Wild Flowers*, which Paxton Chadwick executed for Penguin at W.S. Cowell, six plates were used and the black line was engraved on the ungrained side of the plate. Definition is very good. The colouring is better than is usual even in a much more expensive class of book, and register on the whole is also good. The engraved line suggests the possibility of more use being made by artists of the graver or diamond-point pencil in book illustration. An engraved line has a quality which the pen and ink line, however reproduced, cannot rival. This accounts for the superiority of so many of the nineteenth-century prints. At its retail price (*1s. 6d.*) one can compare it with similar books in the series by the same artist. Kathleen Hale's latest *Orlando* book (*Orlando Buys a Dog*) seems to my eye to be even more vigorous and lively than its predecessors drawn on the zinc, and again she confirms to me her preference for the plastic. Part of one page from this is reproduced here from the original plate by permission of the publishers and printers. I think the first plastic-drawn book to appear in this country was V.H. Drummond's *Flying Postman* in the Porpoise Series, which was printed in six colours and done within two months, including proofs, a feat which stresses the advantages of speed held by this method.

It should be said by the way of cautionary reserve that the plastic plate is not a revolutionary process and opens up no easy road to success for artists. It needs mastering like any other medium, and will not respond to artists who lack the temperament or the patience. Of late there has been a tendency to exalt lithography at the schools, so that students will tell you with hushed pride that they 'do lithography' when they cannot pretend to the most elementary competence in draughtsmanship. No more than the stone or zinc will a plastic plate make a good artist out of an indifferent one.

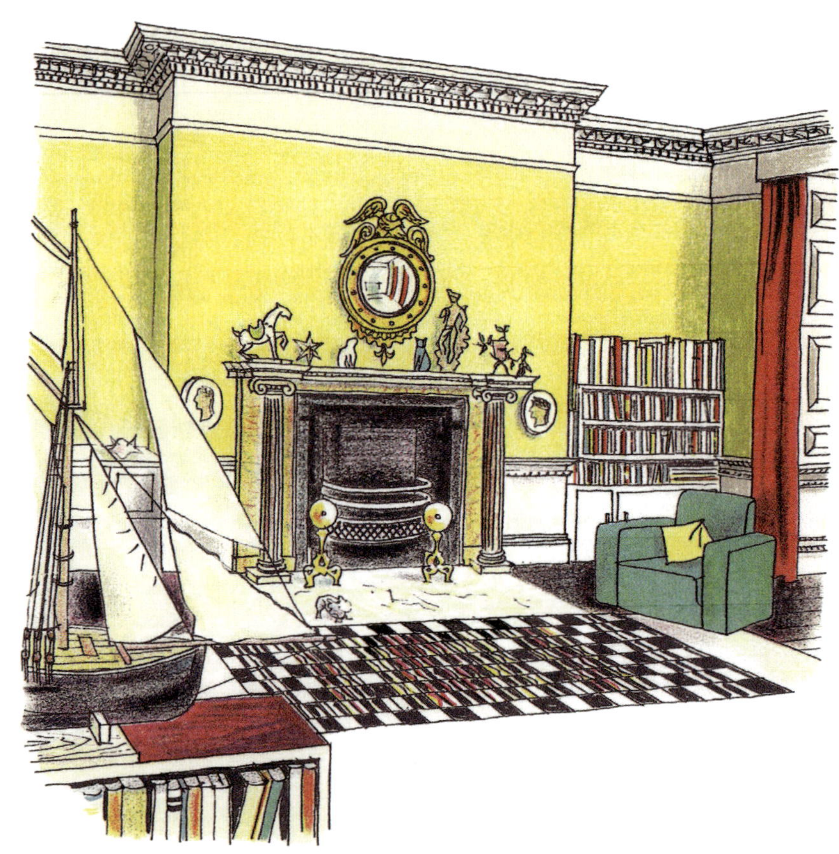

Interior of 29 Percy Street, from Colour and Pattern in the Home

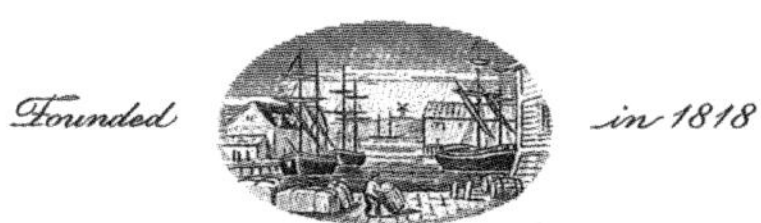

Founded in 1818

W. S. COWELL LTD

BUTTER MARKET IPSWICH

TELEPHONE: IPSWICH 2276 · TELEGRAMS: LITHOCOWL · IPSWICH

Fine Letterpress and Lithographic Printers

The cover design of Do you want it good or do you want it Tuesday?
is adapted from A Handbook of Type and Illustration *by John Lewis,*
printed by W.S. Cowell Ltd, and published by Faber and Faber, 1956

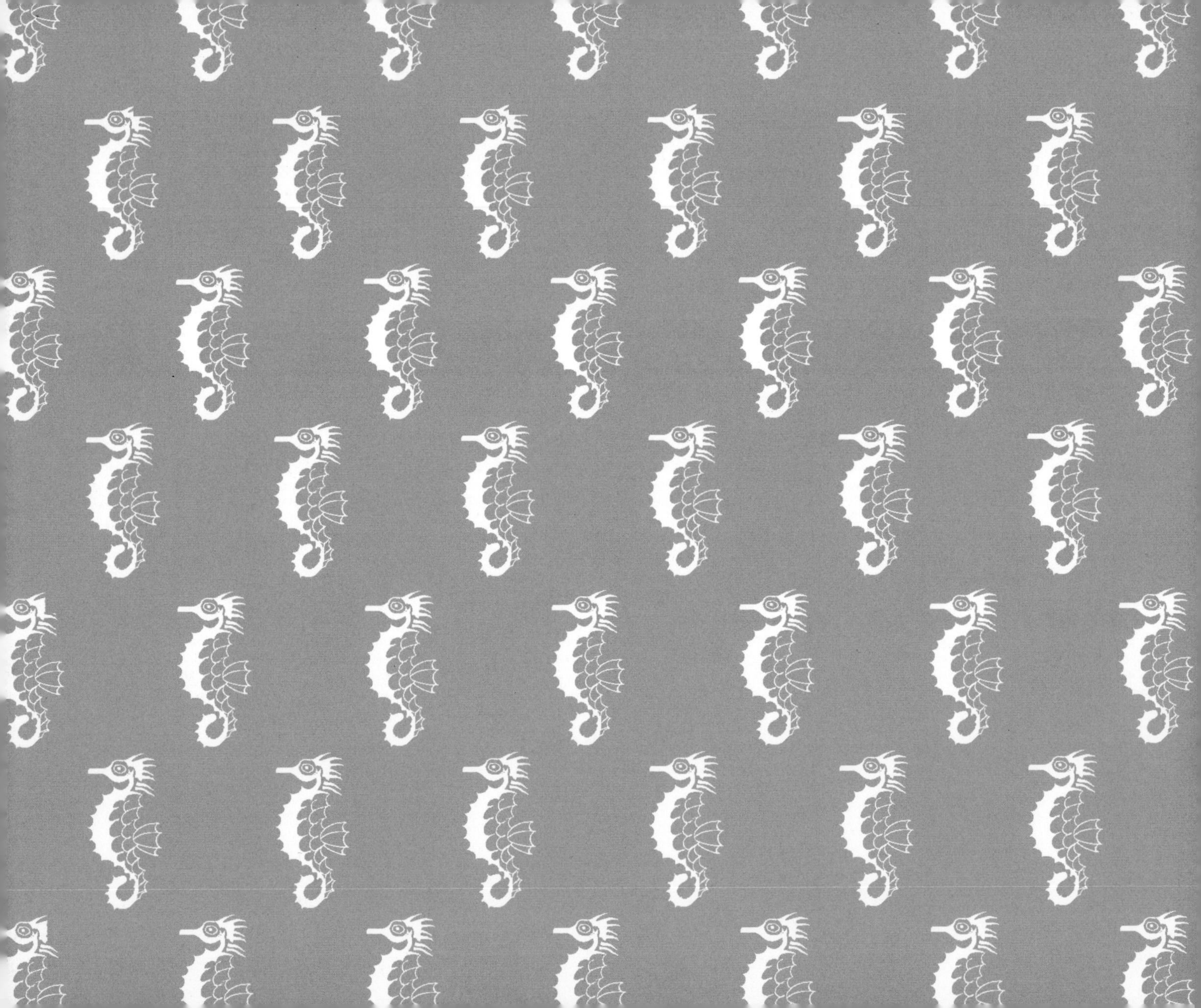